INSIDE THE ANCIENT WORLD

SOCRATES AND ATHENS

INSIDE THE ANCIENT WORLD

SOCRATES AND ATHENS

Meg Parker

MACMILLAN

First published 1973

Published by
MACMILLAN EDUCATION LTD
London and Basingstoke

Associated companies and representatives
throughout the world

PRINTED PHOTOLITHO IN GREAT BRITAIN
BY EBENEZER BAYLIS AND SON LTD.
THE TRINITY PRESS, WORCESTER AND LONDON

Contents

Acknowledgements

The Publishers wish to acknowledge the following sources of photographs:

American School of Classical Studies, Athens   Figs 14, 18, 21

Bibliothèque Royale, Brussels   Fig 5

Trustees of the *British Museum*   Figs 2, 4, 22, 24, 27, 30

Kunsthistorisches Museum, Vienna   Fig 31

The Mansell Collection   Figs 3, 8, 10, 11, 19, 20, 23, 29, 33

Richard Sheridan   Figs 13, 15, 25

Staatsbibliothek, Berlin   Fig 7

Vatican Museum   Fig 6

Victoria & Albert Museum   Fig 32

Figs 9, 16, 26 and 28: photographs taken by the Author.

List of Illustrations and Maps

General Editor's Preface

To get *inside* the Ancient World is no easy task. What is easy is to idealise the Greeks and Romans, or else to endow them unconsciously with our own conventional beliefs and prejudices. The aim of this series is to illuminate selected aspects of Antiquity in such a way as to encourage the reader to form his own judgement, from the inside, on the ways of life, culture and attitudes that characterised the Greco-Roman world. Where suitable, the books draw widely on the writings (freshly translated) of ancient authors in order to convey information and to illustrate contemporary views.

The topics in the series have been chosen both for their intrinsic interest and because of their central importance for the student who wishes to see the civilisations of Greece and Rome in perspective. The close interaction of literature, art, thought and institutions reveals the Ancient World in its totality. The opportunity should thus arise for making comparisons not only within that world, between Athens and Sparta, or Athens and Rome, but also between the world of Antiquity and our own.

The title 'Classical Studies' (or 'Classical Civilisation') is featuring more and more frequently in school timetables and in the prospectuses of universities. In schools, the subject is now examined at Advanced Level as well as at O-Level and CSE. It is particularly for the latter courses that this new series has been designed; also, as in the case of this volume, as a helpful ancillary to the study of Greek and Latin in the sixth form and below. It is hoped that some of the books will interest students of English and History at these levels as well as the non-specialist reader.

The authors, who are teachers in schools or universities, have each taken an aspect of the Ancient World. They have tried not to give a romanticised picture but to portray, as vividly as possible, the Greeks and the Romans as they really were.

Socrates was a controversial figure in his own day and to many people he still remains so. The problem he presents is exacerbated by the fact that he wrote nothing down and that no verbatim reports of his conversations exist. We are dependent on the writings and views of other men: some of these were devoted friends; not a few, on the other hand, thought his influence highly dangerous.

In *Socrates and Athens* Mrs Parker attempts to show us some glimpses of the true Socrates beneath the myth that has grown up around him during the centuries since his death. After a short biographical introduction the author, in a chapter entitled the Questioner and the Quest, discusses such matters as the importance of Anaxagoras, the role of the sophists, and Socrates' sense of divine mission. There follow chapters on life and government in Athens and on Socrates and his friends. The central chapters of the book deal with Socrates' trial, imprisonment and attitude to death, and here quotation from original sources is used as much as possible to tell the story. A final chapter considers the influence of Socrates on his contemporaries and successors.

In the course of her book Meg Parker shows that Socrates asked questions which are as significant today as they were in the intellectual and moral turmoil of fifth century Athens—questions such as 'How can a man attain true goodness?', 'What is meant by a good life?', 'How does one resolve the conflict between freedom of conscience and respect for law and order?'

MICHAEL GUNNINGHAM

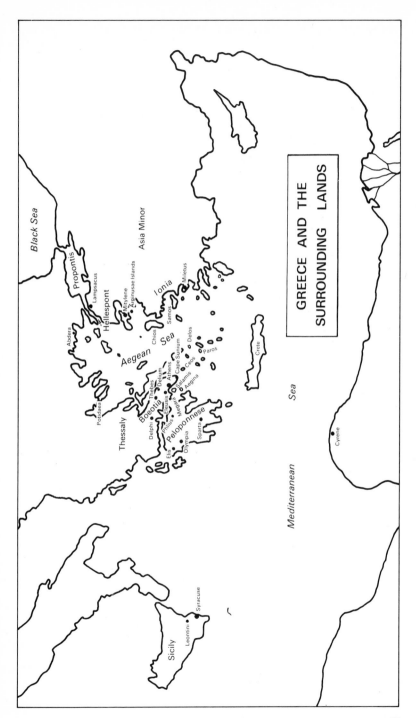

GREECE AND THE SURROUNDING LANDS

Black Sea

Propontis

Lampsacus

Hellespont

Abdera

Mitylene

Arginusae Islands

Asia Minor

Ionia

Miletus

Samos

Chios

Samos

Aegean   Sea

Delos

Cape Sunium

Paros

Ceos

Potidaea

Athens

Salamis

Delium

Thebes   Aegina

Boeotia

Delphi

Eleusis

Megara

Pylos

Peloponnese

Thessaly

Elis

Olympia

Sparta

Crete

Mediterranean

Sea

Cyrene

Sicily

Syracuse

Leontini

2. Socrates

I

Who was Socrates?

The scene: a court in Athens
The date: 399 BC
The speaker: Socrates

> I don't know whether you have been convinced by my accusers, gentlemen; but I myself was almost carried away by them, their arguments were so persuasive. And yet hardly a word of what they said was true. . . . From me, however, you shall hear the whole truth. But don't be surprised if you hear me defending myself in the sort of words I've always used in this city's market-place (where many of you have listened to me) and elsewhere. This is the first time I've come into a lawcourt, and I'm seventy years old; so I'm a complete stranger to the language used here. What I'm asking you is this: take no notice of the kind of language I use, but concentrate simply on whether I'm speaking the truth or not. That is the main duty of a juryman, just as it is the defendant's duty to speak the truth. [Plato, *Apology* 17c]

So, we are told, Socrates began his defence before a jury of five hundred of his fellow Athenians against two charges – corrupting the minds of the young, and sacrilege (or impiety) against the city's gods. According to Athenian custom he conducted his own defence. No verbatim report of the trial exists nor did Socrates himself write down what he said in court. In fact, since Socrates never personally recorded his thoughts or words, we are dependent here, as elsewhere, on the reports of others – and in particular of Plato, a close friend and devoted adherent, some forty years younger than Socrates, whom he met in about 407 BC. Plato's writings have come down to us in the form of dialogues, or dramatised conversations, in many of which Socrates is the principal figure, examining or demolishing arguments of other speakers, or suggesting positive ideas himself. Some of these ideas may have been Plato's, or at least Plato's interpretation of Socrates' views. Indeed, it is impossible to tell exactly how much is Plato and how much Socrates. But in the matter of the trial, there is no reason to suppose that Plato's description of the events – known

3. *Plato*

as the *Apology* – does not constitute a reasonably accurate record. (The Greek word *apologia* simply means 'defence' and does not imply that someone is asking forgiveness for a wrong that has been done.)

Another of Socrates' friends, the general and writer Xenophon, also gives us an account of his trial; but as he was abroad at the time of the case his recollections are not likely to be as trustworthy. Xenophon wrote further reminiscences of Socrates many years later, and these sometimes differ considerably from Plato's. They do, however, help to fill out what we know about Socrates.

Changing Ideas

To understand why a citizen like Socrates should be brought to trial by his fellow-citizens, we shall have to consider how Athenian ideas changed or developed during the seventy years of his lifetime.

In fifth-century Greece a new feeling of enterprise arose with the final defeat of the Persians in 479 BC. Centred in Athens, this feeling grew rapidly during the years when the influence of the statesman Pericles was at its height (446–29). Art, architecture and literature reflected this creative urge, and by the middle of the century the study of physical science, allied with philosophy, had also made great advances. There were so many new ideas that, as in our own day, numbers of ordinary people were finding difficulty in deciding what they ought to believe and by what standards they should govern their lives. Before this, thinkers had tended to concentrate on Nature and the Gods rather than studying themselves and their fellow humans. But now Man was being made the central point of all the inquiries about the world and what happened in it. It was at this time, therefore, that questions of how we ought to live, in other words the study of ethics, began to be thought about seriously.

After the death of Pericles in 429 a new breed of politician emerged in Athens, as the historian Thucydides tells us – men who broke away from the old traditional ways of governing and became very skilful in swaying the opinions of the citizens in order to support their personal ambitions.

> Because of Pericles' reputation, his intellectual powers and his obvious integrity, he managed to keep the people in check while respecting their freedom. It was he who led them, rather than they who led him. He did not have to flatter them, since he did not win his power in the wrong way. On the contrary, as he was so highly respected, he could speak indignantly to them and contradict them. His successors, however, were more on an equal footing with each other, and every one of them wanted the highest position for himself. So they began flattering the people, and they handed over to them the management of affairs of state. As a result, a lot of mistakes were made in a city which had an empire to control. [Thucydides II 65]

It became more important to present an argument well than to have a good argument to present. Established values in morality and religion were attacked, and as Athens became less and less successful in the war she was waging against her old rival, Sparta, and her prosperity declined, the agnosticism and the scepticism of her citizens increased. Things that had previously seemed everlasting were being destroyed and everyone had to begin thinking for himself.

Euripides and the New Learning

One of the leaders of the new thinking was an Athenian dramatist named Euripides who was born about 480. He criticised the established institutions, and for this became unpopular with many of his contemporaries who felt that his views were too advanced. The Theatre is, of course, often accused of *avant-garde* ideas. Euripides took the traditional stories of the gods and heroes as the plots of his plays, but he examined them and revalued them in the light of human behaviour and human problems. He was concerned with the misery of war, the attitude to women, the treatment of slaves, the responsibilities of government, the ways in which power corrupted, and the uncertainties of life. His views were perhaps summed up in the words he put into the mouth of Hecuba, formerly Queen of Troy, but after the Trojan War a prisoner of the Greeks:

> If anyone feels quite satisfied with what he thinks of as his established position in life, he is a fool. The forces that control our lives are as unpredictable as the behaviour of idiots. There is no such thing as certain happiness. [Euripides, *The Trojan Women* 1203]

and in the words with which he ended a number of his plays:

> What we thought would happen does not; the gods make the unexpected possible.

Euripides, the agnostic humanitarian, appeals to an age like our own which is bewildered by changing values. For him, upbringing and education might help in the control of evil, but suffering was inescapable.

Euripides must have known Socrates, who was about eleven years younger. They probably had a great deal in common. Both of them continually questioned established ideas, both tried to examine the nature of truth, love, goodness and justice, and both believed that integrity was the most valuable thing a man could have, and that the spiritual was always worth more than the material. Euripides' unpopularity finally forced him to leave Athens in voluntary exile; Socrates' unpopularity brought him to trial.

Socrates: biographical details

There are few facts known about Socrates' early life. He was born in Athens in 469 BC and Plato recorded in his dialogue *Theaetetus* that his father was a stone-mason and his mother a midwife. It is not clear whether

Socrates followed any trade or profession himself, though he may well have been a stone-mason, too, for a time. We know more about his appearance than his career. He looked uncouth, with pot-belly, bulging eyes, broad nose and a generally bull-like expression. Alcibiades, the Athenian general and political leader and friend of Socrates, remarked at a drinking-party 'Socrates is like a satyr' [Plato, *Symposium* 215], and in an

4. *A Drinking Party* (*Symposium*)

5. *Silenus*

account by Xenophon of another party we read that a friend said: 'If I have no advantage over you in beauty, I must undoubtedly be uglier than a figure of Silenus.' (Silenus was a leering, ugly satyr, symbolising pleasure and wantonness.) To the same friend Socrates later commented: 'Your nostrils are turned downward but mine are wide and turned upward towards heaven'; and 'Don't you think my kisses should be sweeter than yours, as my lips are so thick and large?' [Xenophon, *Symposium* IV and V]

B

Meno, a wealthy and normally self-possessed young aristocrat, remarked in a conversation with Socrates:

> I feel you are using magic and witchcraft, and laying a spell on me until I'm quite helpless. If it isn't too flippant to say so, I think it's not only outwardly but in other ways too that you're like the flat stingray we may encounter in the sea. Whenever a man touches that fish, it produces numbness; and that's what I feel you're doing to me now. [Plato, *Meno* 80 a]

Socrates the soldier

When Socrates was in his thirties he served, like all other male Athenians, in the army. He was a hoplite, that is a heavy-armed infantryman. He would have had to provide his own equipment, and must therefore have had some private means at this time, although at his trial he more than once mentioned his poverty, summing up his position thus:

> Throughout my life I haven't cared about the things most people want, acquiring money and a fine home and high position in army or politics. [Plato, *Apology* 36 b]

He said then that the only fine he could possibly afford to pay was one *mina*. It is difficult to assess the exact value of the *mina* to Athenians in 399 BC. It was not a coin at all, but a sum of one hundred silver drachmas, and its worth varied from time to time. Herodotus, a historian who died about twenty-five years before Socrates' trial, wrote that a prisoner in Greece could be ransomed for two *minas*. In another fifty years or so Plato's pupil, the philosopher Aristotle, assessed such a ransom as more likely to be one *mina*. Perhaps its purchasing power today might be from £50 to £80. If it really did represent Socrates' financial assets towards the end of his life, he was certainly not well-off.

As an infantryman he fought at Potidaea, at the head of the Aegean Sea, between 432 and 429. Alcibiades maintained that Socrates in that campaign was oblivious to hardship and displayed great courage:

> At one time we were fellow-soldiers and were in camp together at Potidaea. There Socrates surpassed everyone in endurance. When, as often happens in campaigns, we had only a few provisions left, no one could put up with hunger like Socrates. In the depths of winter he endured amazing hardships; among other things, while the frost was very severe and nobody went out of the tents much, or if men did go out they wrapped up carefully, Socrates went out wearing only

6. *Alcibiades*

his usual cloak and walked barefoot on the ice. And I ought not to
leave out what he was like in battle. In the engagement after which
I was awarded the prize for courage, Socrates saved my life. He
stood beside me when I fell wounded and saved me from the enemy.
I begged the generals to award the prize to him as he deserved. You
can't deny that, Socrates. But the generals wanted to please someone
of my rank and so they gave me the prize; and you were even more
anxious than they that the honour should be awarded not to yourself
but to me. [Plato, *Symposium* 220]

In 424, when the Athenian army was routed by the Spartans at Delium
in Boeotia, Socrates in retreat once more displayed calm and courage. The
authority is again Alcibiades:

He strutted along with his head in the air, casting sidelong glances,
gazing calmly on both friends and enemies. It was clear to everyone,
even from a distance, that whoever dared to attack him would meet
with desperate resistance. He and his companion got away safely. . . .
Men hesitate to lay hands on those who show such a countenance as
Socrates did even in defeat. [Plato, *Symposium* 221]

Socrates in public life

Socrates never wanted, apparently, to take an active part in public life, but such was the nature of Athenian democracy in which the ordinary citizen shared in the government of his city that he had to do so. In 406 he was chosen by lot to take his turn with other members of his tribe as President of the *Boule*, the Council of the citizens. There had been a great sea-battle at Arginusae, off the Asia Minor coast. In spite of their victory the Athenians lost twenty-five ships, and in bad weather the survivors were not rescued. Not surprisingly there was an outcry at Athens, the commanders were severely censured and were brought to trial on their return. Socrates opposed an illegal suggestion that they should be tried *en bloc*, but he failed to stop their summary execution.

> On that occasion I was the only member who insisted that you, the Athenian people, should not do anything illegal, and I was the only one who voted against the proposal. And although your spokesmen were prepared to lay information against me, and even have me arrested, and you were all encouraging them at the tops of your voices, I felt it was my duty to stick it out on the side of the law and justice, rather than support you in your wrong decision just through fear of prison or death. [Plato, *Apology* 32 b, c]

Two years later, when the war had gone badly and there was a group of thirty men trying to rule Athens, many citizens were asked to help arrest others, so that they might be forced into being accomplices in the government's guilt. Trumped-up charges were common. Socrates was asked to join four citizens who were sent to fetch a certain Leon from his home to be executed:

> I made it quite clear then not by words but by actions that I didn't mind about death at all . . . but I did mind a great deal about not doing anything wrong or unjust. That government, although it was powerful, did not frighten me into doing something wrong. The other four went off to Salamis and arrested Leon, but I went home. I should probably have been executed myself for this if the government had not fallen soon after. [Plato, *Apology* 32 d]

Socrates summed up his attitude thus:

> Do you imagine I should have lived as long if I had taken an active part in public life, and behaving like an honourable man had always defended what was right? Throughout my life I shall be seen to have acted consistently, both publicly and privately, never having agreed to anyone's acting unjustly. [Plato, *Apology* 32 e]

Socrates' domestic life

Although it is possible that Socrates was married twice, the only wife we know about was Xanthippe. She acquired the reputation of being a shrew, and Xenophon records that Socrates himself often referred to her unbearable temper. Antisthenes, another friend, asked in Xenophon's *Symposium* why, if Socrates believed women could be educated just as well as men, he had not trained his wife, but seemed content to live with a woman who was known to be 'the most troublesome of all time'. To that, Socrates answered that everyone realised that a man who trained horses had to practise on very high-spirited and awkward animals and did not concentrate only on docile ones. So, as he wanted to be able to deal with all types of human beings, he had deliberately chosen Xanthippe, knowing that if he could control her, there would be no one he could not handle! It is only fair to add that some writers have defended her, insisting that her bad reputation was all the fault of the same Antisthenes.

Socrates and Xanthippe had three sons, of whom two were still quite young at the time of the trial. She brought them to see their father in prison. At the end of his defence speech Socrates had made a rather surprising request to the Athenians:

> When my sons are grown up, if you think they are valuing money or anything else more than they're valuing goodness, take your revenge by harrying them as I've harried you. And if for no reason they think they are worth something when they're not, you must scold them, just as I've scolded you, for neglecting what is important. [Plato, *Apology* 41 d]

When friends tried to persuade him to escape from prison they promised to look after his children if he left them behind; but Socrates refused to think any more about his sons' lives than his own, and insisted that his only concern was to act according to the standards of honour and justice he had set himself.

It may seem strange that such a man should find himself on trial before his fellow-citizens. But before we consider this question and attempt to answer it, it would be better to examine more closely what Socrates' aims were and the nature of the times in which he lived.

2

The Questioner and the Quest

Fore-runners of Socrates:
Anaxagoras and Archelaus

WE can only guess the stages by which Socrates' ideas developed. He must, however, have been influenced by the progressive thinkers of the fifth century, among whom was Anaxagoras, a philosopher-scientist from Ionia. Anaxagoras moved to Athens about 460 BC and probably spent about thirty years there, becoming a close friend of Pericles. When Pericles became unpopular, Anaxagoras was among those who fell under suspicion, and he only escaped a charge of impiety by fleeing to Lampsacus near the Black Sea – where he was received with great honour. He had asked scientific questions about the nature and constituent elements of the universe, and had suggested that Mind, or Intelligence, had produced order out of chaos. It was when he spoke of the sun as a red-hot stone and the moon as a mass of earth that the Athenian Assembly (under pressure from those who revered both as divine – or pretended still to do so) passed a decree forbidding the study of astronomy as sacrilegious. This action seems to have sparked off the persecution of some intellectuals, though the number was probably small.

To the Greeks sacrilege usually meant robbing or desecrating shrines, or revealing to the uninitiated some secrets about rites and ceremonies. Greek religion was much concerned with ritual. Impiety was, however, a vague notion. A man could be thought impious for speaking blasphemies, but it was not common to attack someone through the legal system just for his beliefs. Plato emphasised in the *Apology* that Socrates' interests were quite different from those of Anaxagoras.

'Do you think you are prosecuting Anaxagoras?' Socrates asked one of his accusers.

> Do you assume these jurymen are so uneducated that they don't know his works are full of these theories? Do the young men really get such ideas from me, when they can from time to time pick them up at the bookstalls for a few pence and laugh at Socrates if he

pretends they're his own – apart from the fact that they're such stupid ideas? [Plato, *Apology* 26 d]

And in another of Plato's works, the *Phaedo*, Socrates complained that Anaxagoras did not attempt to explain how and why the Mind arranged everything for the best:

> I once heard someone reading from a book of Anaxagoras, and saying that it is indeed the Mind that produces order in everything and is the cause of everything. I was delighted by this explanation. And as I thought about it, I was pleased that I had discovered someone who taught about the cause of things and was after my own heart. I never thought that a man who said things were ordered by the Mind would offer any other cause for them than that it was best for things to be as they are. My hopes were quite dashed when, as I read on, I found that he did not attribute the ordering of the universe to the Mind, but just suggested as causes air and ether and water and many other absurd things. It seemed to me he was just about as wrong as if someone said 'Socrates does everything because of the Mind' and then, trying to give the reasons for everything I do, said first that the cause of my lying here now was that my body consists of bones and muscles, the bones rigid and having joints which keep them apart, but the muscles capable of contracting and relaxing, and containing the bones with the help of the flesh and the skin, which holds everything together; and as the bones can move freely at the joints, the muscles in some way by relaxing and contracting make it possible for me to move my limbs; and that is the cause of my reclining here in a bent position! [Plato, *Phaedo* 97c]

Anaxagoras was attacked by the Athenians because of his beliefs and not anything he had actually done. The precedent was set.

There is a tradition that Anaxagoras had a pupil called Archelaus, who was in turn Socrates' teacher. This is based mainly on the words of Diogenes Laertius who lived probably in the early part of the third century AD. He wrote:

> Archelaus of Athens or Miletus . . . was a pupil of Anaxagoras and teacher of Socrates. He was called a physicist and was the first to take physical philosophy to Athens. He also considered law, goodness and justice. [Diogenes Laertius, II 16]

Diogenes was probably wrong about physical philosophy which was more likely brought to Athens by Anaxagoras himself, but he also quoted a near contemporary of Socrates, Ion of Chios, as having said: 'When Socrates was a young man he went off to Samos with Archelaus.' [Diogenes Laertius, II 23]

The Sophists

There was an influential group of men in Socrates' day, known as 'sophists'. They were travelling teachers who went round the cities of the Mediterranean, offering for high fees tuition in the art of eloquence (rhetoric), wisdom and statecraft. Many of them were indeed distinguished scholars, in some respects the founders of higher education. But they incurred hostility because they were 'professionals'. We have to remember that to Athenians such as Xenophon manual labour and earning one's own living were incompatible with intellectual excellence. He reported Socrates as saying: 'Those who for money sell wisdom to anyone who is prepared to buy it are called sophists – or those who prostitute wisdom.' [Xenophon, *Memorabilia* I 6.13]

Since most of the sophists' writings have perished, our chief source of information about them must be Plato. Socrates referred to some of them thus:

> I think it is fine if a man is able to teach like Gorgias of Leontini and Prodicus of Ceos and Hippias of Elis. For such men can go into a city and actually persuade the young to leave their friends and associates, and attach themselves to them, pay to do so and even feel grateful as well. [Plato, *Apology* 19 e]

Hippias taught mathematics, astronomy and handicraft, Prodicus specialised in linguistics, Gorgias in rhetoric. Indeed all the sophists claimed the ability to train their pupils to speak persuasively and argue both sides of a case. Many were sceptics who denied any possibility of universal, unchanging truths, believing that every man was entitled to his own opinion until he could be persuaded to abandon it. Laws were man-made and depended only on the agreement of people to observe them.

Protagoras of Abdera

Protagoras was probably the greatest of the sophists. Even Plato, who disagreed with much of what he believed, treated his views with some respect. He wrote a dramatic dialogue entitled *Protagoras*, which was supposed to have taken place when Socrates was in his thirties. In it Protagoras maintained that a man was the sole judge of his own feelings and beliefs – 'Man was the measure of all things'. What mattered was not a question of truth or falsehood; no one had to consider before trying to make others change their opinions whether he would be persuading them of things that were more true. Similarly, whatever laws a state made were right for it as long as they remained in force, and were just and fair because they were approved by the people.

It would be wrong, said Protagoras, to use violence to try to overthrow the laws, but a wise sophist might by skilful argument persuade a city to change its policies. He believed that all must respect the opinions of others and only when peaceful persuasion failed should punishment be used; even then it must not be considered as retribution, but as one way of educating a man and improving him. This view of punishment is one that many people hold today.

But the main aim of the sophists was to produce successful speakers and politicians. They often turned the heads of their pupils by suggesting that there was nothing that skill in argument would not give them. Most sophists, however, were men of integrity, morally respectable citizens who adhered to the laws of the places in which they lived. Some were shocked by the way their teaching was interpreted and adapted by wealthy young aristocrats, as the doctrine developed that morality was merely a question of the rights of the stronger. Without any evil intention the sophists undoubtedly assisted the breakdown of many old traditions and made themselves unpopular with those who wanted to cling to them.

Socrates, on the other hand, insisted that goodness, justice and courage really existed and must be understood before an action could be judged right or wrong. This was one of the central themes of Plato's major work on education and society, the *Republic*. By attacking the sophists' doctrines by means of Socrates' arguments, Plato helped to give the sophists themselves a bad name. Sophistry now implies false argument with intent to deceive. But it could be said that without the sophists the Greeks could scarcely have had a Socrates.

Socrates' aims

There were those who accused Socrates of being a sophist himself, partly because he tried to show people the limitations of their knowledge. But Socrates was never a professional teacher nor did he receive any fees. His chief aim was to find a better alternative than cynical immorality as an answer to the problem of how a man could live a good life.

Before his time the *psyche* (which we now translate as 'soul') had meant 'breath of life', a vapour essential for the survival of the human body. But once that body died, all that was left of the *psyche* was a feeble shadow. A few of the earlier thinkers had gone beyond that, suggesting that the *psyche* might be part of an eternal and divine fire, or even that it was a god temporarily dwelling in the body. None, however, had yet developed any idea of the soul as the intellectual and moral force which made a living man a real person. Socrates believed it was the centre of a human being's ability to reason things out. Yet even the soul could not always be rational, that is, reason properly. Man had to struggle to become his true self and see that the rational part of his soul was permanently in control of the irrational. Socrates (or possibly Plato – it is difficult to be certain) was perhaps the first man in the western world to have a clear idea of the soul as a responsible agent in knowing what was right and wrong and acting accordingly. He considered that the care of the soul was the highest human activity and that the individual was important. This was one of the most decisive developments in the history of human thought.

The Delphic Oracle

At Delphi, which the Greeks considered to be the centre of the world, was a shrine and oracle of Apollo. Apollo was the god of light (later being identified with the sun), medicine, music, archery, and especially prophecy. Through his oracle at Delphi Apollo gave advice to any who cared to consult him and could make the necessary offerings. His priestess, the Pythia, while in a trance, uttered incoherent words which were interpreted by priests in the form of verses, often of ambiguous meaning. Gradually these priests had built up a store of information gathered from inhabitants of all parts of the Mediterranean who visited the shrine. But the ultimate responsibility for the oracular replies was always believed to be Apollo's.

7. *Apollo's priestess, the Pythia, being consulted by a king.*

8. *Apollo*

Over the shrine were written the words 'Know yourself'. Socrates made these his own maxim, insisting that true knowledge cannot be imparted by anyone else, but must be acquired in and for oneself.
He said at his trial:

> I have never been a teacher of anyone; but if anyone, young or old, wants to listen to me talking, I have not grudged him this. [Plato, *Apology* 33 a]

According to Plato, as we have seen, Socrates' mother was a midwife and Socrates liked to think of himself as a midwife too, concerned with minds and souls in labour instead of bodies. 'Apply to me as to a midwife, a son practising his mother's art,' Plato recorded him as saying in the dialogue *Theaetetus*. Man must always examine himself and his thoughts and be helped to do so. His accusers might advise him to mind his own business, but this he could not do.

> This is the hardest thing of all to make some of you understand. If I say that it would mean disobeying the god and that is why I cannot keep quiet, you will not believe that I am being serious. But suppose I say that it really is to a man's advantage to have a discussion every day on the subject of goodness and the other things you hear me discussing and asking questions about, both of myself and of others; and that the unexamined life is not worth living. If I emphasise this, you will be even less likely to believe me. [Plato, *Apology* 38 a]

Although they might refuse to take him seriously and might become angry with him to the point of condemning him to death, Socrates felt that he must continue to examine the lives of others and the standards men set themselves to live by.

Chaerephon, a friend of Socrates from childhood, had enthusiastically gone one day to consult the god Apollo at his shrine and, according to Socrates:

> He dared to ask the oracle if there was anyone wiser than I; then the priestess answered that there was no one. When I heard this, I began to think, What does the god mean? Why is he speaking in riddles? I'm well aware that I'm not wise in any great or small degree. Whatever does he mean by saying I am the wisest man? He cannot be lying; that would not be right for him.' [Plato, *Apology* 21 b]

At the beginning of the war with Sparta, the Delphic Oracle had seemed

9. *Remains of the Temple of Apollo at Delphi*

clearly anti-Athenian. According to Thucydides, who wrote a history of the war:

> The Spartans sent to Delphi and enquired of Apollo whether it would be wise for them to fight. The god replied, so it is said, that if they fought with all their strength they would be victorious, and he himself would be with them, whether they called on him for help or not. [Thucydides, I 118]

The Athenians therefore began to have the feeling that whatever happened, the god of Delphi would be hostile to them. Euripides in two plays written in the early years of the war, *Andromache* and *Ion*, pointedly attacked Apollo and his advice. In another play also, *Hippolytus*, written in 428, in an outburst generally taken to refer to Apollo, Hippolytus cried: 'If only a human being's curse could affect a god!' [Euripides, *Hippolytus* 1416] Political considerations in Greece would inevitably affect the lives of private citizens. Could it have been that the apparent approval of Socrates by Apollo's oracle contributed to the distrust and dislike of him by some Athenians?

In 401 Xenophon was invited to go to Asia Minor with the chance of serving under Cyrus, the claimant to the Persian throne. He was clearly attracted to the idea, but consulted Socrates first. Socrates suggested he should go to Delphi for advice. This Xenophon did and discovered from Apollo to which gods he should pray and sacrifice so that he might have a safe journey and be successful. He reported later in his *Anabasis* that on his return from Delphi he went again to Socrates, who blamed him for not having first asked whether it would be better to go or stay at home. He added, however: 'But as you have asked the question in this way, you must do what the god has ordered.' [Xenophon, *Anabasis* III 1.5] Obviously Socrates, while recognising that certain rules had to be followed in the business of consultation, sincerely trusted the ability of the Delphic Oracle to give divine guidance.

Socrates' sense of divine mission

In an attempt therefore to find out the truth of Apollo's reply to Chaerephon, Socrates began to question all kinds of people who had the reputation of being wise. He first approached a politician, but, not surprisingly, incurred resentment by trying to show him that he only thought he was wise and seemed so to others, whereas in fact he was not. Despite the reaction he met, Socrates' sense of divine mission drove him on to interview many others with a similar reputation for knowledge. 'You must see my travels as those of a man performing labours only to find the oracle quite unable to be refuted.' [Plato, *Apology* 22 a] He next questioned the poets and discovered that they composed only as a result of inspiration, like prophets, and that they possessed no wisdom which enabled them to write.

> And at the same time I realised that because of their poetry they thought they were the wisest of men in other respects as well. So I went away from there, too, feeling that I had the same kind of advantage over them as I had over the politicians. [Plato, *Apology* 22 c]

Finally, after questioning expert craftsmen he came to the conclusion that their technical skill led them to claim complete understanding of every subject, however important.

> This error of theirs seemed to overshadow the knowledge they might have. As a result, I asked myself on behalf of the oracle whether I would rather be as I was, not wise with their kind of wisdom nor ignorant with their kind of ignorance. I replied to myself and to the oracle that it was to my advantage to be as I was. [Plato, *Apology* 22 e]

The resentment he stirred up grew and remained, in spite of his final conclusion that Apollo was not literally referring to Socrates as one

10. *Potters and a vase painter*

11. *Shoemaker at work*

person, but was taking his name as an example of those few wise people who realised the limitations of their own knowledge.

> This is why I still continue my search and enquiry, in accordance with the god's command, when I think there is any citizen of Athens or foreigner who is wise. And if I find one who is not wise, I help the god by demonstrating the fact. Because of this occupation I have had no time to do anything worth mentioning in politics or in my own private affairs; but through my service to the god I am in a state of extreme poverty. [Plato, *Apology* 23 b]

All this seems to show Socrates' sincerity and piety (if he really was serious about the Delphic Oracle; could he perhaps have had his tongue slightly in his cheek?). Perhaps the story of the prophetic voice he claimed to hear also indicates a true belief in guidance from a god. This voice opposed him whenever he was likely to take a wrong course of action, although it did not encourage him to do anything positive. Not that there is any indication that he believed, in the way St Joan of Arc did, that he had any special or direct communication with a supernatural being. It is much more as if he felt he possessed a kind of 'sixth sense' about the possibility of bad luck, and as a result was able to draw back from disaster in time.

Socrates was always concerned with human beings. Men had, of course, to live in relationship with each other and with whatever was eternal in the universe. So he was constantly talking about and enquiring into the nature of truth, goodness, love, friendship, immortality and 'justice'. Particularly 'justice', which had for the Greeks a different meaning from that which it has for us. The Greek word *dike* originally implied only 'custom' or 'usage', and from that developed the idea of 'what was fitting or right' and then of 'goodness'. Socrates and Plato linked justice with lawfulness and suggested that those who acted as the law demanded were the just members of the community. For this reason, although Socrates thought that Athenian law made a mistake in condemning him, he felt he should conform to what had been decided.

When he considered justice or talked about it, he would begin to examine closely the way his fellow Athenians behaved as citizens as well as individuals – in other words, their political behaviour. The Greek word *polis* (the city state) was used to express what the Athenians of the fifth century felt to be the finest form of association among human beings. It was natural, therefore, that it should be in the *polis* that they and Socrates hoped to find truth and justice in the end.

The Athens in which Socrates lived and the ways in which he and his friends set about discovering the truth about Man and his standards of conduct, will be discussed more fully later in this book. But it is worth noting now that so closely was the name of Socrates associated with new ideas and changes of attitude, and so quickly did he himself become something of a legend, that the Greek thinkers who preceded him are known collectively as the 'Pre-Socratics'.

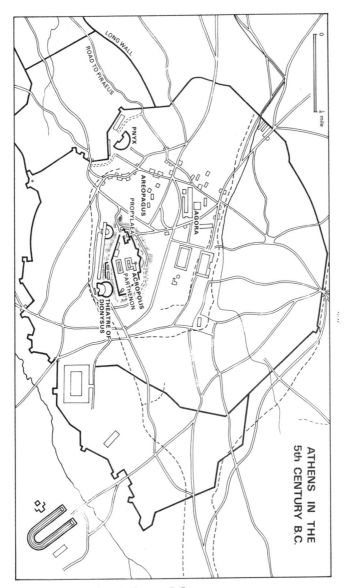

12. *Plan of Athens in the 5th Century BC*

3
Athens in Socrates' Day

Results of the War with Sparta

By 400 BC Athens' pride was crushed. Thirty years of almost continuous war and disturbance had ended in Spartan victory. The Athenians had tried to maintain an empire of those they euphemistically called their 'allies', but had finally capitulated in 404. By the terms of the peace treaty they lost all their foreign possessions, while remaining independent; they gave up their fleet, and they agreed to demolish the Long Walls and fortifications built between the city and the harbour of Piraeus some four miles away. In addition, all exiles were to be allowed to return.

Now the Athenians were to become allies of Sparta. Not everyone was despondent at this situation. Those who had disapproved most of the government were delighted at the opportunity now presented to overthrow it with the help of Sparta and the returning political exiles.

CRITIAS

The most prominent of these exiles was Critias, who had been a pupil of the sophist Gorgias and a former friend of Socrates. He was an orator and politician as well as a poet and philosopher, and an avowed atheist. Now he was appointed one of thirty men whose task was to redraft the laws and supervise affairs at Athens until this was completed. The 'Thirty', as they came to be known, in turn chose a group of Eleven for secret police duties – to assist in purging Athens of wrongdoers. Inspired by motives of revenge, fear and greed, some of them instituted a reign of terror with the intention of ridding themselves of possible rivals, and at the same time acquiring their property and possessions. It was during this period, when many Athenians were expected to help round up their fellow-citizens, that there occurred the incident which was referred to in Chapter 1 – when Socrates refused to assist in the arrest of Leon of Salamis.

Another of Socrates' friends had also become unpopular with a considerable number of Athenians. This was Alcibiades, a handsome, talented man, but in the eyes of many staid citizens a rather disreputable character. In 415 Alcibiades, then about thirty-six years old, had been chosen as one of three generals to command an expedition against Sicily. On the eve of its departure a number of statues of the god Hermes were found

13. *Square pillar with bust of Hermes*

mutilated. (These were square pillars with a bust of Hermes on top which it was customary to set up at street corners and in front of houses throughout the city.) Alcibiades was accused by his enemies of being implicated in the outrage. He was allowed to leave for Sicily as planned, but on his arrival there he was summoned to face further charges – this time of sacrilege in connexion with the secret cult of the goddess Demeter at Eleusis. Managing to escape during the journey back to Athens he made his way to Sparta, where he gave valuable advice to the enemy. Later he intrigued with the Persians. He was condemned to death in his absence by the Athenians who confiscated his property as well.

Four years after, however, Alcibiades was recalled and pardoned in the hope that he would be able to obtain an alliance with Persia. After eight years in exile he went back to his native city where he was enthusiastically received. Solemnly released from the curse laid upon him for his alleged profanation, he was appointed commander-in-chief of the Athenian forces. Restitution, however, was short-lived. In the same year an Athenian fleet was defeated by the Spartans off the coast of Asia Minor. Though he was not personally present at the battle, Alcibiades was held responsible and once again relieved of his command. This time he went to the Hellespont region, at the entrance to the Black Sea, an area of strategic importance to the Athenians. He made one more attempt to help them. In 405 he warned them that there was danger to their fleet in that region, but his advice was ignored and the Athenians suffered a serious defeat at the hands of the Spartans. When the Thirty came to power and banished him yet again, he took refuge with Pharnabazus, a Persian governor of Phrygia, in Asia Minor. On his orders Alcibiades was assassinated.

His association with Critias and Alcibiades did Socrates little good. Socrates may have saved the latter's life at Delium in 424, but the hatred felt by many Athenians for Alcibiades and his activities contributed twenty-five years later to the prejudice and ill-will which deprived Socrates of his own life.

The Government of Athens

Twice in Socrates' lifetime, in 411 and 404, there were revolutionary attempts to overthrow the government of Athens and transfer authority from the many to the few. But during most of his seventy years the citizens were expected to share in the responsibilities of governing their city. Every male Athenian of eighteen and over had the right to attend the *Ecclesia* (Assembly). Obviously only a fraction of the total number would be present at any one of the meetings, which were probably held every ten days or so. Those who were there on each occasion constituted the

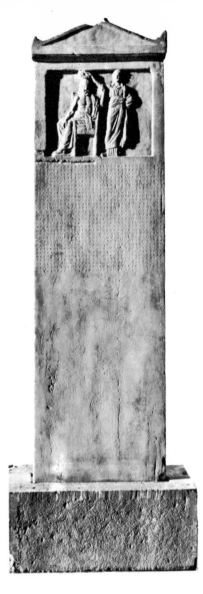

14. *Democracy places a wreath on the head of Demos*

demos; in other words, for that meeting they were considered as being the People, and their decisions were therefore recognised as those of the whole citizen-body. Similarly the juries in the courts, chosen by lot from a panel of six thousand Athenians, were felt to be the *demos* in legal matters.

Business for the *Ecclesia* was prepared by the *Boule*, a Council of Five Hundred, chosen annually by lot. All adult males were eligible, but probably no one could be a Council member more than twice in his lifetime. The Council provided on a rota basis the President of the Assembly for the day. There were, in addition, large numbers of officials, most of them chosen by lot. All Athenian officials, of whatever status, were responsible directly to the People, as represented by Assembly, Jurymen or Council.[1]

Participation in the work of governing was thus widely shared among the citizens. But many of them might not always have understood the intricate business of foreign policy or financial affairs, and to an increasing extent Athens would depend on a number of able individuals prepared to devote themselves to politics. Among such men there would often be tension, and there was always the risk that the *demos* might become impatient and resentful at failure, as happened after the Battle of

[1] For a fuller discussion see R. Barrow, *Athenian Democracy: The Triumph and the Folly*, in this series.

15. *Democracy crowning Demos*

Arginusae. On such occasions the efforts of someone like Socrates to restrain the Athenians' anger were hardly likely to achieve much.

The City of Athens

The climate of Athens and the nature of the fifth-century city encouraged the inhabitants to spend much of their life in the open air. Athens had been considerably improved during the time of Pericles in his attempt to make her the Queen of Greek cities. The Parthenon, the marble temple in honour of the patron goddess Athene (the *Parthenos* or Maiden), had been built on the Acropolis and there were several other shrines built there or restored at this time. Pericles, in fact, spent so much money on projects of this kind that he was accused of appropriating some of the contributions of the allies to pay for them.

Down the slopes of the Acropolis to the south-east lay the precinct of the god Dionysus; it contained two temples, an altar and a portico, but the greater part of it was occupied by an open-air theatre in which were held the dramatic festivals. In these festivals Socrates would certainly have seen the plays of Sophocles and Euripides (who both died in 406) and of Aristophanes (who survived him by nearly twenty years).

16. *The Parthenon*

THE AGORA

Below the Acropolis was the market-place, the *agora*, which was the centre of Athenian life. The administrative buildings, courts of justice, shops, orators' platforms and more temples and shrines were here. Just below the temple of Hephaestus stood most of the official buildings. One of these was called the *Tholos*, a round building which served as a State Dining Hall where free meals were offered to the councillors, guests of honour and Athenian victors in the Olympic Games. When Socrates at his trial was asked to propose his own penalty, he suggested he deserved a reward instead:

> What is appropriate for a poor man who is helping you and needs leisure so that he can go on encouraging you? I can't think of anything more appropriate for such a man than free dinners in the State Dining Hall. He deserves them much more than someone who's been victorious in the Olympic Games. That sort of man makes you *think* you're fortunate; I make you really so. He doesn't need your support; I do. [Plato, *Apology* 36 d]

In the centre of the *agora* was a large open space. Among the trees and in the porticoes surrounding it, fifth-century Athenians walked and talked with their friends.

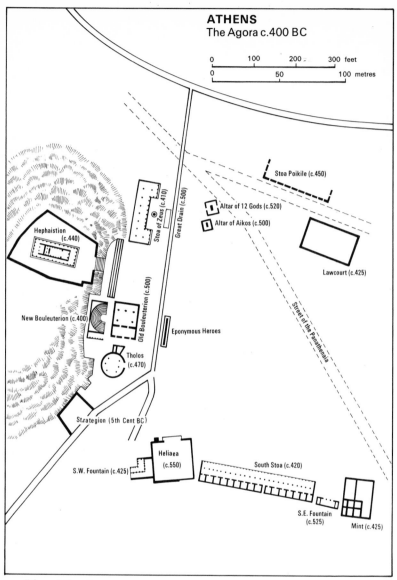

ATHENS
The Agora c.400 BC

| 0 | 100 | 200 | 300 feet |

| 0 | 50 | 100 metres |

Stoa Poikile (c.450)

Stoa of Zeus (c.410)

Great Drain (c.500)

Altar of 12 Gods (c.520)

Altar of Aikos (c.500)

Hephaistion (c.440)

Lawcourt (c.425)

New Bouleuterion (c.400)

Old Bouleuterion (c.500)

Eponymous Heroes

Street of the Panathenaia

Tholos (c.470)

Strategion (5th Cent BC)

Heliaea (c.550)

South Stoa (c.420)

S.W. Fountain (c.425)

S.E. Fountain (c.525)

Mint (c.425)

17. *Plan of the Agora*

BEYOND THE AGORA

To the south-west lay the *Pnyx*, which was the hill near the Acropolis where the Assembly met. There was a flat open space with a speakers' platform and a natural amphitheatre formed by the surrounding slopes.

18. *The speakers' platform on the Pnyx*

Here, too, Socrates and his fellow-citizens gathered for discussion and argument, both official and unofficial. Between the Pnyx and the Acropolis the *Areopagus* (the Supreme Court) and the *Boule* held their meetings on the Hill of Ares, named after the god of War.

Of the great gates in the city walls the finest was the *Dipylon* (Double Gate) through which led the road to Piraeus harbour and the grove of olive trees called the Academy, where Plato and his successors taught.

The Athenians' love of talking

Such was fifth-century Athens. Because its minor streets and private houses were often dark and uninviting, the citizens tended to meet in the market-place, gymnasium or wrestling-ground, at performances in the theatre or during processions to the temples. They would talk informally, in groups, in a sociable and friendly way. Pericles in his Funeral Oration in honour of Athenians killed in the war with Sparta commented:

> We carry on our political life freely and openly. Other men are frequently suspicious of each other in their day-to-day activities. But we are not angry with our neighbour if he does what he pleases, nor do we give him disapproving looks, which, although they may not actually harm people, do hurt their feelings. [Thucydides, II 37]

In such groups Athenians might discuss or argue about most of the matters that concern us today – law and morality, religion, man's technical achievements and the distribution of wealth. It was here that Socrates would be found in conversation and argument with his friends. The Greek word *dialegesthai*, meaning 'to have a conversation with someone', was the origin of 'dialectic', a term used to. describe the method of argument he adopted. It was particularly suited to him, and through his skill it became a strenuous process of question and answer in an attempt to discover the truth.

4

Socrates and his friends

MANY of Plato's Dialogues bore the names of Socrates' friends – for example Charmides, Euthyphro, Laches, Meno, Crito and Phaedo. Crito was probably his closest and oldest friend, a kindly, practical man who took part in several of these dialogues. He watched over Socrates and is best remembered as the spokesman of those who wanted Socrates to attempt escape from prison. (He failed to persuade him, for reasons which will be discussed later.) There was a story that Phaedo, whose name Plato gave to the dialogue containing the account of Socrates' last hours, had come as a prisoner of war from Elis and that, at Socrates' instigation, his freedom had been bought for him either by Alcibiades or by Crito and other friends.

In the *Apology* several others are mentioned. In addition to speaking of Chaerephon who had consulted the Delphic Oracle, Socrates pointed out in the court the fathers and brothers of some of the young men he was accused of leading astray, people who might have been expected to stand up and testify against him, but did not:

> Certainly many of them are present here, as I can see for myself; first Crito, the father of Critobulus, then Lysanias, the father of Aeschines, and Antiphon, the father of Epigenes; and over there are other men whose brothers have been in this circle of ours, like Nicostratus, the brother of Demodocus and Paralius. And here's Adimantus, son of Ariston, whose brother Plato is over there. . . . And there are many others I could mention. [Plato, *Apology* 33 e]

Socrates and his friends would gather spontaneously for discussion. Such a meeting is described by Plato at the beginning of the *Republic*. Socrates tells how he had been down to the Piraeus on the previous day with Glaucon to take part in a festival and watch a procession:

> We were making our way back to town when Polemarchus saw us in the distance and sent his slave running on ahead to ask us to wait for him. The slave grabbed hold of my cloak from behind and said, 'Polemarchus wants you to wait!' I turned round and asked him

19. *Philosophers talking*

where his master was. He answered, 'He's just coming along behind you; do wait for him.' 'All right, we will,' said Glaucon. And not long afterwards Polemarchus caught us up. With him were Adimantus, Glaucon's brother, Niceratus, the son of Nicias, and several others who'd all apparently been watching the procession. Polemarchus said, 'Socrates, I imagine you're setting off on your journey back to town.' 'That's right,' I answered. 'Do you see how many of us are here?' he asked. 'Yes, of course.' 'Well, you'll either have to get the better of us all or stay where you are.' 'But there is another alternative; we might succeed in persuading you to let us go,' I said. 'You can't persuade people who won't listen to you,' Polemarchus replied. And he added, 'There's going to be an all-night carnival as well, and that will be worth seeing. We'll all go out after dinner to watch it. We'll meet a lot of young men there we can talk to. Please stay.' Glaucon turned to me and said, 'It looks as if we'll have to.' 'All right,' I said, 'If you think so, we will.' [Plato, *Republic* 1 327]

So they all made their way to Polemarchus' house, where they found a number of people already together. Most of them were young men, but Cephalus, Polemarchus' father, who was very old, was also delighted to see Socrates and gently reproached him for not coming there more often:

20. *Aristophanes*

'You don't come down to the Piraeus as often as you should, Socrates. If I were strong enough to come into town I'd visit you. But since I can't do that, you ought to visit me more frequently. I find that old age dulls my enjoyment of physical pleasures, but my need for intelligent conversation and my enjoyment of it are increasing!' 'As a matter of fact, Cephalus,' I answered, 'I like talking to very old men. They've gone on ahead of us, so to speak, along the road we'll most probably have to tread ourselves, and I think we can discover from them what it's like, and whether it's rough and hard or wide and easy.' [Plato, *Republic* 1 328]

There must have been many others who at various times thought of Socrates as their master and were proud to be known as his disciples. Some are mentioned by Xenophon, who contrasts them with the pupils of the sophists:

> Chaerecrates, Hermocrates, Simmias, Cebes and Phaedondes, who with the rest who followed him, did so not to become popular orators or pleaders in the lawcourts, but honourable and good men. [Xenophon, *Memorabilia* II 48]

Aristophanes

It is difficult to know whether to include Aristophanes the comic playwright among Socrates' friends, or to think of him rather as an enemy. Plato represented him in his *Symposium* as a pleasant and amusing companion who gave a humorous turn to a serious discussion about Love. (Aristophanes talked of himself in that dialogue as an entertainer, and began with a fantasy of the nature of the first human beings, asserting that men were only halves of original wholes, and that Love was their attempt to unite themselves with their lost halves.) But in his comedies Aristophanes attacked new ideas of all kinds – though it would be unwise to label him as conservative in outlook on these grounds. His political plays certainly indicated that he supported the landowners and farmers, and vigorously opposed war policies which brought suffering and hardship to them. However, he mocked all the leaders in turn and caricatured contemporary customs and ridiculous or bad individuals of all kinds.

A favourite subject for his parody was any fashionable intellectual movement. One of these was the 'sophistic' philosophy with which he associated Socrates and the so-called New Learning. In his comedy the *Clouds* (first produced in 423) a certain Strepsiades suggests that his son Pheidippides should enrol as a pupil in Socrates' school (called the *Phrontisterion* or 'Think-Tank'); the idea is that the boy should learn how to make the worse and weaker argument always defeat the better, and thus they should find a way of cheating their creditors. When the son refuses, Strepsiades himself becomes a student, and first catches sight of the Master swinging high up in the clouds in a basket:

> STREPSIADES: What *are* you doing? Please tell me.
> SOCRATES: I'm walking about in the air, allowing my thoughts to move round the sun. . . . I couldn't have made my remarkable discoveries about things above the earth without suspending my

thoughts and blending them with the pure atmosphere. To make elevated enquiries from down on earth would ruin my theories. [Aristophanes, *Clouds* 224 ff]

The sophists are shown in this play as cranks and cheats who, as well as wasting their intellectual powers on scientific trifles, destroy both religion and established morals by introducing new gods. By unscrupulous argument they corrupt the minds of the young, making them lose any respect they had for their elders. At the end of the play the Think-Tank is burned down, and it is implied that no one would have been worried if its master Socrates had gone with it.

This was clearly a false picture of Socrates. But he was a familiar figure in Athens, poor, shabby and ugly, an obvious victim and the easiest of the intellectuals to attack. His methods were unorthodox, and it was natural that in the minds of many Athenians who saw the *Clouds* he should be linked with the 'new-fangled nonsense' which they blamed for many of their misfortunes. Plato certainly felt that Aristophanes was responsible for the public outcry against Socrates some twenty-four years after the play was produced. In the *Apology* he referred to it thus:

> You have yourselves seen this in the comedy of Aristophanes. There Socrates is swinging about, saying he's walking on air and talking a lot of similar nonsense about things I [Socrates] know nothing at all about. I am not speaking disparagingly of such knowledge, if anyone really is expert in such matters . . . but I myself am not concerned with them. [Plato, *Apology* 19 c]

Socrates and Plato

As has already been suggested in Chapter 1, the beliefs of Socrates and Plato were inextricably entwined. It is likely that at first the dialogues in which Socrates was represented as taking the leading part were fairly true records of conversations he actually had. As time went on, Plato interpreted Socrates' views much more, and then his own theories were put into Socrates' mouth. Gradually Socrates became a minor character in the dialogues and finally did not appear at all.

It is clear that Plato used artistically the material he possessed. He did not just report facts or words, but he did know Socrates well, and he would have been unlikely to invent a purely fictitious figure of him. Nobody would maintain that there was at any point a clear break where Socrates' ideas ended and Plato's began; it is rather a matter of how they merged in a steady process of development. Plato was Socrates' most famous disciple, and like Socrates he had the power of making people *want* to find out the truth.

Plato was probably quite young when he first met Socrates, who by this time was devoting himself entirely to considering questions of ethics and was going round the city asking people what exactly they meant by words like 'justice', 'goodness' and 'self-control'. Plato comments that he himself had thought that politicians were going to reform society and had watched their activities with deep interest. But he soon became disillusioned about politicians and turned with relief to those who seemed to be asking the right questions, and to Socrates in particular.

THE 'FORMS' OR 'IDEAS'

Socrates had insisted that absolute moral goodness did exist and that men could only become good through their knowledge of it. Thus it followed that someone would act rightly because he knew what was right, and would not voluntarily do wrong. But Socrates himself had not tried to define this 'goodness'. Plato accordingly attempted to discover its true nature. He suggested that there was an eternal world of realities which he called 'Forms' (sometimes rather misleadingly called 'Ideas'), which could not be perceived by man's senses, but only by his mind. There were, for example, eternal Forms of the Just, the True and the Beautiful.

THE 'REPUBLIC': THE MYTH OF THE CAVE

When Plato felt that his arguments might be difficult to follow, he made use of a myth. In the *Republic*, written about twenty years after Socrates' death, there is one of these myths which sounds remarkably like an allegorical version of the Athenians' reaction to Socrates, although it is included to explain men's reaction to the theory of universal Forms. Plato describes a cave in which live imprisoned creatures who have never seen the daylight of the outside world:

> They have been prisoners there since childhood, their legs and necks chained so that they are only able to look straight in front of them. Some way above them and behind is burning a fire, and between the prisoners and the fire is a track, in front of which a parapet has been built, like a screen for a puppet show in front of the audience. [Plato, *Republic* VII 514]

He further describes how the prisoners, facing this wall, see on it the shadows of people and objects passing outside, and in their ignorance assume that these shadows are the real things. Suppose at last one prisoner were taken out into the sunlight and, full of wonder at reality, should return to report to his fellows still inside that cave and try to drag them out to see. Would they not be likely to resist him and, believing him mad, even kill him?

Plato also showed Socrates attempting to separate justice from injustice in both society and the individual. In so doing he first traced the growth of a state from a tribal society, and then suggested how in a truly just community there must be efficient government. This led him to consider the importance of higher education for the young 'Guardians' of the state, as he called them. This must be made up of carefully censored cultural pursuits, together with strict but simple physical education. The rulers, or 'philosopher-kings', would be recruited from this group and would have to become professional philosophers, the only citizens able to approach nearest to the eternal Forms of Truth, Goodness and Justice. To free them to pursue philosophy, all productive work would be the task of craftsmen.

Such views expressed in the *Republic* were almost certainly Plato's own, though the speaker was Socrates. Many of these views seem distasteful to modern readers, who feel that a state of that kind would be too organised, too controlled, too much subject to censorship for any real freedom on the part of the individual. But Plato did pose clearly a problem faced by all civilised communities:

> Unless philosophers achieve kingly power or those we now call our rulers become sufficiently inspired with a desire for true wisdom . . . neither nations nor, I believe, mankind, can ever be free of trouble. [Plato, *Republic* v 473 c]

Furthermore, in old age he wrote:

> I at last came to the conclusion that all existing states were governed badly. I was forced to believe that the only way of discovering justice for society or for the individual was by way of philosophy. [Plato, *Letters* vii 326]

In some ways the *Republic* represented Socrates' life and his search for truth. In Plato's view the true philosopher *was* Socrates, and he never forgot what Socrates taught, that wisdom can only begin when an individual discovers that he does not really know what he *thinks* he knows. Part of Plato's purpose in that dialogue was surely to stimulate his readers to question their own beliefs about man and society, and propose alternatives when they disagreed with his, just as Socrates had always insisted that the unexamined life was not worth living.

D

5
Trial

Prejudice against Socrates

IT is not difficult to see why prejudice against Socrates had grown over the years. The charge of leading young citizens astray must have come readily to the minds of those conservative Athenians who, suspicious of new ideas and bewildered and disillusioned at their city's change of fortune, were looking for someone to blame. Socrates was well aware how dangerous to him such men were.

> Over a long period many people have come forward to accuse me and tell you lies about me. . . . They constitute a greater danger, gentlemen, because they got hold of a number of you when you were young. They made utterly false accusations against me then in their attempts to convince you. They said, 'There is a clever man called Socrates, who thinks about things up in the heavens and investigates everything below the earth; he also succeeds, when he's discussing, in making the weaker argument appear the stronger'. It's these people who have thrown scandal at me and are really dangerous. They've used envy and slander and they're very difficult to deal with. I cannot possibly bring them into court to cross-question them or refute their charges. I have to defend myself just as if I were boxing with shadows. I have to argue my case without anyone here to answer me. [Plato, *Apology* 18 b]

Further hostility was aroused against Socrates as a result of his efforts to discover the meaning of the Delphic Oracle's response. As he himself admitted, this hostility was

> of the most trying and painful kind, and it has led to a lot of prejudice against me. It has caused me to be labelled 'Wise-man', because every time I prove someone else is not wise on some subject or other, my listeners think that I am expert in that subject myself. [Plato, *Apology* 23 a]

There was, he added, another reason for his unpopularity.

> A number of wealthy young men with plenty of time to spare follow
> me around of their own accord. Because they enjoy hearing people
> cross-questioned, they often imitate me and try to cross-question
> others. I am sure they have no difficulty in discovering hundreds of
> people who believe they have some knowledge when they really know
> little or nothing. As a result of this, those questioned get angry not
> with themselves but with me, and say that there's a villain called
> Socrates who leads young people astray. When anyone asks them
> what he does or teaches, they can say nothing and are at a loss; but
> so as not to appear in difficulties, they make use of the stock charges
> against all philosophers. [Plato, *Apology* 23 c]

Socrates had felt he was undertaking a divine mission when he carried
out his questioning of citizens. He described himself as a stinging fly sent
to stimulate the city 'as though it were a huge, thoroughbred horse, which
because of its size is rather sluggish and needs to be stirred' [Plato,
Apology 30 e]. He said that, like the fly, he continuously settled here and
there, rousing, persuading and reproaching each one of them. Horses do
not like being stung by flies, and the Athenians did not like being 'roused,
persuaded and reproached' by their divinely (or self-) appointed stinging
fly. It did not soothe them to hear that Socrates had neglected his own
material well-being, and that of his family, in order that he might urge
everyone else towards goodness.

The charge of impiety

The second part of the charge against him is less easy to explain.
Addressing one of his accusers Socrates said:

> Surely it is clear from your indictment that you accuse me of teaching
> them (the young) not to believe in the gods the State believes in,
> but in other strange gods. [Plato, *Apology* 26 c]

From this he argued that he could not therefore be a complete atheist
but was obviously being accused because he encouraged belief in *different*
gods. A prosecutor who admitted this but at the same time insisted that
Socrates was an atheist, was contradicting himself and could not be taken
seriously. Everyone who believed in the activities of horses must believe
in horses; everyone who believed in musical activities must also believe
in musicians. Therefore everyone who believed in the activities of supernatural beings must believe in supernatural beings themselves.

What then was the meaning of this charge of impiety? Socrates could not have been convicted of lack of belief in myths about the gods. Probably few Athenian intellectuals in his day really believed in them. Greek religion lacked orthodoxy; demands were not made for respectful treatment of the gods. Aristophanes, for example, not only made fun of Dionysus, the very god in whose honour the dramatic festivals were held, but also of Zeus, the King of the Gods; and Aristophanes survived. Many foreign deities, like Cybele from Asia Minor, were being brought into Athens with official approval at this time. Socrates was not accused specifically of encouraging their worship; and it is not likely that the Athenians would have minded if he had been. Probably he neither believed nor disbelieved in the existence of the generally accepted gods. The question of their existence would have seemed to him of little importance compared with his quest for truth and justice; it was these that he thought of as the very foundation of religion.

Xenophon suggested it was Socrates' 'divine voice' on which his accusers based part of their case, but there is no satisfactory evidence to support this. Even if there were substance in this suggestion, 'divine voices' were not unacceptable to the Greeks, who paid great attention to prophets, oracles and soothsayers.

It is probable that Xenophon's account of the trial was less trustworthy than Plato's (after all, he had not been present in court). It is interesting, however, that in Xenophon's version Socrates challenged the prosecution to name anyone he had been guilty of turning from piety to impiety. The reply came that it was possible to name many whom he had persuaded to obey his authority rather than that of their parents. To this Socrates countered that that was surely a question of *education*, in which one must always look to the experts. In other words, it was not in matters connected with the *gods* that he could be faulted.

The true reasons for the charges

Admittedly Socrates was unpopular with many Athenians. He was eccentric and behaved very oddly at times, even to the point of falling into a trance. Alcibiades described him in the *Symposium* as standing a whole day and night in contemplation, oblivious of the fact that his fellow-soldiers were watching him. He tended to irritate people because, tenacious in argument, he would put them in a dilemma about their principles and standards of conduct. He had a sense of humour which his enemies certainly did not appreciate, and which might have been regarded during his trial as contempt of court. However, none of these faults was really enough to bring about his downfall. Political reasons must also have contributed to it.

Any male Athenian citizen over the age of thirty could be a juryman and each of the ten tribes had to provide an annual list of six hundred jurymen chosen by lot. The six thousand Athenians thus chosen would be assigned

21. *Machine for choosing jurymen by lot*

to different kinds of cases. Usually about five hundred citizens would try any one case, though it could occasionally be two or three times that number. At Socrates' trial the jury consisted of five hundred and one Athenians. There was no professionally trained presiding judge; any state official might be asked to act as chairman of the court. No skilled lawyers were there to plead on behalf of their clients, though speech-writers did exist and their services could be hired in advance of the case. An interesting conversation was recorded in a book called *The Lives and Beliefs of Eminent Philosophers*, probably written in the third century AD and bearing the name of Diogenes Laertius. There is no proof, of course, that this conversation actually occurred, but it would have been in accordance with the views Socrates expressed at the beginning of Plato's *Apology*.

Lysias, the professional, writer had apparently prepared a defence speech for Socrates, who read it through and said, 'It is a very splendid speech, Lysias, but it won't do for me; it is obviously the speech of a lawyer, not a philosopher.' When Lysias retorted, 'Why won't it suit you if it's a good speech?' Socrates answered, 'It won't suit me any more than fine clothes or beautiful shoes would.' [Diogenes Laertius 40]

The State did not prosecute its citizens, but it was the duty of all to see that criminals were brought to court. The Athenians at that time seem to have enjoyed litigation, either bringing charges against each other, or sitting as jurymen in order to draw their daily fee of two or three obols—a poor wage but one on which it would have been just possible to exist.

22. *Three obol piece, depicting Athene and the owl (a symbol associated with both the goddess and Athens)*

Because of this love of the lawcourts, a severe fine might be imposed on anyone who brought a false or flippant charge that could not be satisfactorily upheld in court.

Speeches were of limited length, timed by a *klepsydra*, or water-clock, and the proceedings were expected to be completed in a day. The jurymen sat on benches and listened to the prosecution's case first. When the defendant had replied to the charges, their voting shells or pebbles were dropped into one of two urns – for condemnation or acquittal. If there were no fixed penalty for the crime being dealt with, a second vote would be taken after conviction to decide on one. A proposal could be made by either side. It might be a fine, loss of citizenship, exile or death. Long terms of imprisonment were not favoured. One common form of capital punishment was fastening the condemned man to a board which had holes for the head, arms and legs, setting it up outside the city, and leaving him to die in agony, perhaps over a period of several days. Death by poisoning was considered almost a privilege, rather like being allowed to commit suicide. Voluntary exile frequently enabled a man to avoid the prescribed sentence and was particularly useful if he could not pay a huge fine.

A Water Clock (Klepsydra)

23.

Modern lawyers and judges use highly specialised and professional methods in court and seem to have an unfamiliar, secret language of their own. In England a jury of twelve ordinary members of the public is there to ensure that the accused is tried by his fellow-citizens. In Athens the entire business was in the hands of those citizens who constituted for each trial the *demos*.

24. *Juryman's ticket*

In June 1970 American archaeologists working in the Athenian *agora* discovered in the north-west corner a building which they identified as the Stoa of the Basileus. It was sixty feet long and twenty feet wide, with columns on the two long sides, and it contained on the north wall some benches of stone on which Socrates' judges may well have sat. It was here that the city's nine annually elected *archons* (or governors) met. The name of the building came from the *Archon Basileus*, a title given to the official in charge of religious affairs, dramatic festivals and the administration of justice.

SOCRATES' ACCUSERS

One of Plato's dialogues opens with a conversation between Euthyphro and Socrates:

> EUTHYPHRO: Socrates, what has made you leave your haunts in the Lyceum [a gymnasium and garden outside Athens] to wait here round the Stoa of the Basileus? You're not, like me, bringing a charge against someone, are you?
>
> SOCRATES: No, Euthyphro. The Athenians don't call it bringing a charge, but facing one.
>
> EUTHYPHRO: What do you mean? Someone, I suppose, has brought a charge against *you*? You are not going to tell me that you've brought a charge against someone else.
>
> SOCRATES: No, indeed.
>
> EUTHYPHRO: Then someone *has* accused you?
>
> SOCRATES: Precisely.
>
> EUTHYPHRO: Who is it?
>
> SOCRATES: I don't really know the man very well myself. His name is Meletus, I believe – if you can recall a Meletus of Pitthus, lanky-haired, hooked-nose, with a sparse beard.
>
> EUTHYPHRO: I can't, Socrates. But what's the charge he has brought against you?
>
> SOCRATES: Charge? Rather a grand one, I think. It's no mean achievement for a young man to have learned about these things. He says he knows how the young are led astray and who the people are who corrupt them. He must be a clever chap. Seeing my stupidity in corrupting his contemporaries, he goes off to accuse me to the State, as though he were running to his mother.
>
> EUTHYPHRO: Tell me, what does he say you're doing to lead young men astray?
>
> SOCRATES: Some extraordinary things, my friend. He says I am the creator of gods, and it is for creating strange gods and not believing in the traditional ones that he's charged me. [Plato, *Euthyphro* 1 a]

The lanky-haired Meletus was possibly a young poet or the son of a poet. It was he who actually pinned up the notice charging Socrates and proposing the death penalty. He may have been representing those writers whom Socrates had approached and annoyed during his examination of so-called 'wise Athenians'.

A professional orator named Lycon was another of his accusers, but nothing much is known about him. There is no doubt that the man who really led the prosecution was Anytus, a well-known and responsible democratic statesman. The fact that he became involved in the case suggests that Socrates was not prosecuted in any light-hearted way. On the contrary, the charge was the result of careful thought and sincere belief. Socrates and his ideas were, to citizens like Anytus, a possible danger to the constitution; he had therefore to be removed.

We find hints in other works of Plato that the real reason for Socrates' condemnation was his criticism of Athenian democracy. Once when the statesman Callicles said to him: 'You ought to be the servant of the state', Socrates had replied, 'Don't tell me that my life should be at anyone's mercy, for if that's so, I repeat I shall be an innocent victim; and don't say that my possessions will be confiscated; if they are, the confiscator will get nothing.' Callicles had then warned him: 'Socrates, you appear to be as sure that this won't happen to you as if you lived in another world and were not likely to be taken to court.' [Plato, *Gorgias* 521 c]

In the dialogue called the *Meno* it was Anytus himself who delivered the warning after Socrates had criticised democratic heroes:

> I think you are too ready, Socrates, to run people down. If you listen to my advice you will watch your step. I expect that in all cities it is easier to hurt a man than to help him, and it's certainly so here, as you yourself doubtless know. [Plato, *Meno* 94 e]

Xenophon suggested that Anytus also had a personal grudge against Socrates. He wrote:

> It is reported that when he saw Anytus go by, Socrates said, 'There goes someone who openly admits that it would be a fine and glorious thing if he had me put to death. I had once remarked, you see, that when Anytus had been honoured with some of the most important offices in Athens, it was wrong of him to bring up his son just to follow the family trade of tanning.' [Xenophon, *Apology* 29]

Whether the cause was personal or political or both, clearly it was Anytus who was behind the charges facing Socrates.

The Verdict

The main points of Socrates' defence speech have already been referred to. It may be helpful, however, to summarise them here:

1. He began by speaking of his past and present accusers and the charges laid against him.

2. He denied that he was ever a professional teacher like the sophists.

3. He had interviewed his fellow-citizens to try to discover the meaning of Apollo's oracle.

4. He put down his unpopularity to his questioning of people and to his young followers' imitation of his methods.

5. He insisted that any harm he might have done the young was completely unintentional. A man should not be brought to court for doing wrong unintentionally but should be privately reproved.

6. He was convinced that the only thing which mattered was the knowledge that he was acting rightly, even if his actions endangered his life. On the few occasions when he had taken part in public affairs he had had the courage to stand by his principles.

At the end of his speech he said he had no intention of bringing his family into court to excite pity, as was frequently done by defendants.

> You are much more likely to condemn a man who stages such mournful scenes – and makes the city look ridiculous – than one who keeps quiet. [Plato, *Apology* 35 b]

His last words before the jurors voted were: 'I assign to you and God the task of judging me in whatever way is best both for me and for you.'

25. *Jurymen's ballots*

Two hundred and eighty of the jury cast their votes for condemnation, two hundred and twenty for acquittal.

Allowing for the fact that the fee might have attracted a good many poor men to act as jurors, and that rich citizens who could easily afford the time might also be there in considerable numbers, this was probably a reasonable cross-section of Socrates' fellow citizens. If their views did fairly represent those of the whole citizen-body, then the closeness of the voting suggests that feelings in the city were divided about him and the danger he constituted. However, many jurors who were undecided at the beginning of the trial would have had bitter memories of the events of the last thirty years. Almost without realising it, they may have gained the impression during the trial that in Socrates they were seeing an embodiment of the ideas which had helped to bring about those events.

SOCRATES' COUNTER-PROPOSAL

Even after his conviction, Socrates' humour did not desert him. With the irony for which he was well known, he argued that the three accusers had each individually won a third of the 280 votes cast against him – that is, ninety-three. Now one of the ways of discouraging frivolous lawsuits was to fine a prosecutor who did not achieve one-fifth of the total votes cast, which on this occasion would have meant, of course, a hundred votes. Socrates must have enjoyed his own illogical reasoning when he remarked that if Anytus and Lycon had not joined in, Meletus would have had to pay a fine of something like £50. He continued in the same vein, suggesting that he personally deserved not punishment but a reward – free dinners at the State's expense, such as victors in the Olympic Games received. Even when he condescended to mention an actual penalty, he suggested just one *mina* – which was, he said, all he could afford. As we have already noted, the present purchasing power might be from £50 to £80. Socrates' offer was hastily amended by his friends Plato, Critobulus and Apollodorus, to thirty times that amount on their security.

But the jury voted for the death penalty.

HIS FEELINGS ABOUT DEATH

If the prosecution had thought that the prospect of dying would upset Socrates, they soon discovered their mistake. He insisted that the real problem was not how to escape death but how to escape wrongdoing. It was his accusers, he said, who were more at fault and on whom punishment would eventually fall.

> There will be plenty of people who will condemn you – those whom so far I have kept in check, although you didn't know it; and, as

they are younger, they will be harder on you and cause you more trouble. You are deluding yourselves if you think that by killing me you will stop anyone denouncing you for wrong living. You can't escape that way. The best and easiest way is not to silence others, but for every one of you to make himself as good as he can. [Plato, *Apology* 39 d]

In case they were still unconvinced that he did not fear death, he told them that dying must either be like a perpetual night of dreamless sleep – and all would agree that that should not be unpleasant – or a removal to another world. If the latter, he might expect to find there the dead heroes of previous centuries. He himself would be delighted to have the chance of talking to them and questioning them, just as he had questioned the living.

There was one other important aspect of his condemnation. His 'divine voice' had been completely silent and had made no attempt to dissuade him from coming to the court. Therefore what had happened to him must be something good; had it been bad, he would have had warning. Those who thought that death was an evil could not possibly be right.

Then, after asking the Athenians to see that his children grew up to care more about doing right than living safely and acquiring possessions, Socrates spoke his last words to the court:

Now it is time for us to go away, for me to die and for you to live; but which of us is going to a better condition is not known to anyone except God. [Plato, *Apology* 42 a]

6

Imprisonment

The ship from Delos

ALTHOUGH an Athenian sentence of execution was usually carried out immediately, Socrates stayed in prison for a month. The circumstances were abnormal. It happened that his trial occurred on the first day of the annual mission to the island of Delos in the Aegean, about a hundred miles from Athens. Delos was sacred to the god Apollo, whose birthplace it was believed to be, and his temple there had long been a religious centre. This mission was meant to commemorate the legend of Theseus' killing of the Cretan bull-monster, the Minotaur, to whom an annual tribute of young Athenian men and women had been sent. The Athenians had vowed when Theseus left for Crete that if he were successful in destroying the Minotaur they would send a sacred embassy to Delos every year. They faithfully kept this vow. While the sacred ship was away on its errand, Athens was considered to be in a state of ceremonial purity and no execution was allowed to pollute the city. Plato wrote:

> The mission begins when the priest of Apollo puts a garland on the stern of the ship, and this happened on the day before the trial. That is why Socrates had such a long time in prison between his trial and his death. [Plato, *Phaedo* 58 c]

According to Plato in the *Phaedo* (though not in the *Apology*) Socrates' old friend Crito had offered to go bail that Socrates would not try to escape in the time between the trial and the return of the ship. When Socrates was talking about death to his companions on their last visit to him in prison, and was trying to comfort Crito, he remarked:

> You will have to be surety to Crito for me, as at the trial he was surety to the jury for me – but it will have to be a different sort of surety. For he guaranteed that I would stay in the city; you, on the other hand, must guarantee that I shall not. And then Crito won't take my death so badly. [Plato, *Phaedo* 115 d]

Crito's news

Crito was one of Socrates' regular visitors for more than three weeks. The warder had become used to seeing him. One morning he even admitted him before dawn, when, depressed and unable to sleep, Crito felt he must at once take Socrates his news of the ship's imminent arrival. When he entered the room he was surprised to find the prisoner sleeping calmly and comfortably in spite of the chains fastened round his ankles. Crito sat down at the foot of the bed for a while, watching until Socrates should stir. As soon as Socrates woke he guessed the reason for his friend's early visit – his period of imprisonment must be almost at an end. Crito told him that some Athenians who had just arrived from Cape Sunium (about thirty miles south of Athens) had caught sight of the

26. *Cape Sunium*

sacred ship on its way back from Delos. It would certainly reach the Piraeus before the day was over and the sentence of execution, Crito said, would be carried out a few hours after its arrival.

Socrates, however, was not convinced about this last point. He told Crito he had just been having a dream in which a beautiful woman dressed in white had said to him, 'You will come to the delightful land of Phthia on the third day'. This he interpreted as meaning he would not die till two days later. Plato did not attempt to give any explanation of the dream.[1]

Crito was not prepared to discuss this dream, but was anxious to emphasise that many people would blame Socrates' friends – and that included himself – for failing to persuade the prisoner to escape. He was afraid, he said, that he would be considered mean and contemptible because he seemed unwilling to spend money on Socrates' behalf:

> 'Most people will fail to be convinced that you refused to escape although we pressed you to do so.'
> 'But my dear Crito, does the opinion of "most people" matter so much? The *best* people, who require more consideration, will think that things happened exactly as they have.'
> 'But Socrates, you yourself see that popular opinion does matter. The present state of affairs clearly proves that when somebody gets a bad reputation the mass of the people is able to cause trouble not just in unimportant ways but to an almost unlimited extent!' [Plato, *Crito* 44 c]

Socrates countered this by saying that he wished people did have an unlimited capacity for doing harm, since they might then have an unlimited capacity for doing good as well. What in fact they did was act at random, without rhyme or reason.

OFFERS OF HELP FOR SOCRATES

So Crito tried once more to bring the conversation on to a practical level. Could it be that Socrates thought his friends would suffer at the hands of informers if they helped him to escape, and would then themselves have to pay fines or lose their possessions? If so, he need not worry. There were men ready to get him out of the country for a fairly modest fee. Besides, informers could always be bought off quite cheaply. Crito mentioned non-Athenians who had already brought money which could be spent on this – among them two Thebans named Cebes and Simmias – in case Socrates felt unprepared to endanger the lives of his fellow-citizens by using their resources.

Socrates indeed had many foreign admirers, as we discover from the following references. The philosopher Aristotle, a pupil of Plato, reported that Socrates once refused an invitation to visit the court of Archelaus,

---

[1] Modern editors have suggested that Socrates might have had Phthia in Thessaly in his mind because he remembered Homer's reference to the Greek hero Achilles 'going to his home in Phthia' and had thought of death as going to *his* true home. It has even been suggested that there is a connexion here – possibly subconscious on Socrates' part – with the Greek word *phthio*, meaning 'I perish'.

King of Macedon; from Plato's dialogue *Phaedo* we learn that a certain Echechrates of Phlius (a town in the north-eastern part of the Peloponnese) who was unable to be in the prison during Socrates' last hours, was anxious to receive a reliable account of what took place on that occasion. After Echechrates had begged Phaedo to list those of Socrates' Athenian friends who were present, he asked:

> 'Were any foreigners there too?'
> 'Yes, Simmias of Thebes, and Cebes and Phaedondes, and Euclides and Terpsion from Megara.'
> 'Were Aristippus and Cleombrotus there?'
> 'No; it seems they were in Aegina.' [Plato, *Phaedo* 59 c]

Now Aristippus was a native of Cyrene, and had come all the way to Athens from North Africa because of Socrates' reputation. During the war with Sparta, the cities of Megara, Thebes and Phlius were cut off from Athens, but clearly Socrates' admirers who lived in those places did not forget him; they came to see him again as soon as peace was made and travel to Athens was possible once more. It may be that the doubts about Socrates' loyalty to his native city that had been voiced by people like Anytus were confirmed by the very speed with which men recently classed as enemy aliens came to visit him after the war. Crito certainly believed that there were plenty of places where Socrates could take refuge, and he specifically suggested that he had personal friends in Thessaly who would offer a warm welcome.

But to return to the conversation with the prisoner. When Crito saw that none of his words so far had had much effect, he tried a different approach. He mentioned Socrates' sons, and accused him of planning to desert them and make them orphans when he had it in his power to finish their education elsewhere; this plea, too, fell on deaf ears. Finally, with a mixture of anger and despair, Crito reproached Socrates for taking the easiest way out, instead of making a brave and good choice; and *he* was the one who had always insisted that the only thing that mattered was goodness. His friends were ashamed and embarrassed by the whole business. First there had been his determination to stand trial, when he could have gone away before the case ever came on; then there was the way he conducted his defence in court; and now they were faced with the ludicrous situation of his refusing to consider escape. He had one night left in which to change his mind – he *must* be reasonable and listen to advice, now, at the very last moment.

SOCRATES' REACTION TO CRITO'S REPROACHES

It is not difficult to imagine Crito, exhausted after this appeal, and unable to think of any further arguments, looking hopefully at his friend Socrates for some sign of agreement. But there was no hint of it yet. Socrates thanked him for the warmth of his feelings but insisted that the questions raised must still be very carefully considered. Surely Crito would admit that one should not value the opinions of all men, but only of some men – the opinions, that is, of good men? When Crito agreed to this, Socrates continued:

'When a man is in serious training, does he listen to the praise, criticism and opinions of everyone, or only those of one person – his doctor or trainer?'
'Only of one person.'

27. *Athlete with discus and trainer*

'Then he ought to be afraid of the criticism and welcome the praise of just that one person and not of the general public?'
'Obviously.'
'So he ought to act and train and eat and drink in the way thought right by that one person who is his instructor and an expert, rather than according to the views expressed by everyone else?'

E

'Yes, that's right.'

'And if he disobeys that one person and ignores his opinion and his praise, and pays attention to the views of the majority who are not experts, won't he suffer harm?'

'Of course he will.'

'What harm? And what part of the man who is disobedient will it affect?'

'His body, clearly. That's what is harmed.'

'Good. Now tell me, Crito, is this also true of the matters we're discussing – questions of right and wrong, honourable and dishonourable, good and bad? Should we follow the opinions of the majority and mind about them rather than those of the one expert?'

[Plato, *Crito* 47 b]

Socrates pursued this line of reasoning until he persuaded Crito to accept that they must consider the rights and wrongs of an attempted escape from justice. The points which Crito had raised about Socrates' duty to his friends and his children, and about popular opinion were, he insisted, of no real importance. The only thing that mattered was the rightness or wrongness of the action they finally decided to take. Crito conceded this point, but maintained he was still not clear in his own mind whether Socrates in attempting escape would be breaking agreements he had made with the State. To help him, Socrates suggested that they should imagine the laws of Athens as personified beings who could come to argue with them. This may sound a rather far-fetched idea, but it was quite a familiar one to the Greeks. In addition to their gods and goddesses, Muses, Fates and Furies, they personified such things as grace, old age, peace and victory. Therefore to think of the 'Laws' of Athens as participants in a dialogue would not, for Crito, be either strange or difficult.

THE VIEWS EXPRESSED BY THE LAWS OF ATHENS

The first argument that might be put forward in such a discussion would be that any adult citizen who decided he did not like the organisation of the State was quite free to go elsewhere. But if he remained, it must be assumed that he undertook to obey the Laws, which acted as parent, guardian and adviser. Since Socrates had rarely left Athens except on military service, he appeared to approve of her constitution. An attempt to escape would indicate that he was prepared to act against her Laws and break the contracts he had as a citizen made with them.

The question of his place of exile would next be examined. Well-governed states nearby might be reluctant to accept him, regarding him as a possible destroyer of law and order. Thessaly, which had been mentioned, was notorious for laxity, indiscipline and luxurious living, and it would be like attending a perpetual orgy to make one's home there. But would Socrates continue his discussions about goodness in such surroundings? Could he consider taking his children there? Or did he propose to leave them behind for friends in Athens to educate? If so, why should he think the same friends would refuse to look after his sons if he went away not to Thessaly but to the next world?

The Laws might sum up their case thus:

> Socrates, listen to us, your guardians, and don't pay more attention to your children or to your life or to anything other than what is right; so that when you go to the world of the dead you may have all these pleas to make in your defence before those in authority there. . . . But if you go away in dishonour, repaying injustice with injustice and wrong with wrong, breaking your agreements and contracts with us and hurting those who least deserve it – yourself, your friends, your country and us its Laws, then *we* shall be angry with you while you are alive and our brothers there, the Laws in the next world, will give you a hostile reception, knowing that you tried your best to destroy us. So follow our advice rather than Crito's. [Plato, *Crito* 54 b]

This was the way Socrates supposed the Laws might argue against his friends' appeals to escape. He said that he could hear the sound of the Laws ringing in his ears, just as the worshippers of Cybele, the Asiatic mother-goddess, were known to hear the ritual music of the flute long after it had ended. The voice of the Laws, indeed, excluded all other ideas that might be put into his mind; it would be quite useless for anyone to suggest a different point of view. Nevertheless Crito could try again if he really felt there was any point in further discussion. Crito could only reply: 'I have nothing to say.'

Socrates' final words suggested his true feelings. When he said: 'Let us act in this way, since it is the way God directs,' he surely implied that the imaginary voice of the Laws was to him another form of that 'divine voice' which prevented him from taking a wrong course of action. Yet the whole argument as he propounded it is not perhaps quite as straightforward and logical as it would appear at first sight. He had said one should despise the views of the majority of the people. At the same time he insisted that he must adhere completely to the laws of the State. Who had made those laws but the majority of the Athenian citizens? Crito, however, did not see any illogicality, or, if he did, he was too distressed to comment on it. When he, with other friends who had joined him later, finally left Socrates in the evening, the news was definite. The ship from Delos had reached Athens. Socrates had one more day to live.

28. *Delos*

7
Death

His last day in prison

I T is in Plato's *Phaedo* that we are given an account of Socrates' last hours on earth. From that dialogue we learn of the discussion Socrates had had with a group of his friends, and of the manner of his death. It appears that as the group left the prison on the evening before, they had heard that the sacred ship had just arrived back from Delos, and so they urged one another to meet at the usual place as early as they could in the morning. On arrival they were told by the gaoler to wait, since State officials were inside, taking off Socrates' chains and warning him that his sentence must soon be carried out.

When they were admitted they found Socrates' wife Xanthippe sitting with her husband, their youngest child on her knee. The arrival of his friends made her cry out that it was the last time they would be able to talk with him; then she broke into hysterical weeping. Socrates looked at Crito and said: 'Crito, one of you had better take her home.' Some of Crito's slaves thereupon led her away. Socrates sat up, and as he began massaging his leg just released from the fetters, he talked of the pain he had been suffering and the pleasure he now felt after the pain was gone.

Cebes interrupted with a message from Evenus, a sophist and poet from the island of Paros, who wanted to know why Socrates had suddenly decided in prison to try his hand at poetry – a version of Aesop's fables and a Hymn to Apollo. Socrates answered that he had often had a dream in which he was encouraged to cultivate the Arts. Although he had previously interpreted the Arts to mean in his case Philosophy, he thought that now being near to death it would perhaps be safer to practise a more popular form of art. He asked that this reply be communicated to Evenus, together with a message of farewell, and the advice to follow Socrates as quickly as he could.

A philosopher's attitude to death

This led to a lively discussion about the rights and wrongs of suicide, until Crito broke in with a warning from the Governor of the prison that talking excitedly and becoming overheated might affect the action of the poison to be administered later. If, however, he thought that that would make Socrates keep quiet, he soon discovered how mistaken he was. Just pausing to say, 'That's his business; he must be prepared to give me the poison two or three times if necessary,' Socrates launched into a dialogue about death and the attitude of philosophers to it.

His friends agreed that when a man died, his soul was released from the shackles of the body. So a true philosopher would never concern himself with the delights of food, drink, fine clothing and sex, which other men thought important, but would try as far as possible to free his soul from the distraction of physical pleasures while he was still alive. We know, of course, that Socrates himself did not worry about money, clothes or anything approaching luxurious living, although he did on occasion enjoy a banquet and could stay sober much longer than most people; certainly he seemed to find little difficulty in keeping his body completely under control. In this he perhaps underestimated the problems of others. As we have seen, his powers of endurance as a soldier had amazed Alicibiades and the rest of the army on campaign with him. Not everyone would feel able to go as far as Socrates when he said:

> The body fills us with loves, lusts, fears, every kind of fancy and a lot of nonsense, so that because of it we can never really think about anything at all. Wars and revolutions and battles are caused only by the body and its desires. Wars occur because people want to acquire wealth and we are forced to acquire wealth because of the body, since we serve it like slaves. It's for these reasons that we have so little time for philosophy. Worst of all, if we do have any time free from physical demands and begin to pursue some line of thought, the body always interrupts us, confusing and disturbing our enquiries and preventing us from ever seeing the truth. We know by experience that if we are ever to have pure knowledge of anything, we must rid ourselves of our bodies. The soul in itself must look at things in themselves. It seems therefore that we shall not be able to attain wisdom (which we are eager to have and say we passionately desire) until we are dead. [Plato, *Phaedo* 66 c]

So if a man had trained himself always to live his life as free as possible from the claims of his body, surely it would be ludicrous for him to be upset when death came and deprived him of his physical existence altogether?

The attainment of true goodness

Moreover, Socrates argued, the philosopher was the only really brave and controlled person. Whereas most people were courageous merely in order to enjoy greater pleasures, the philosopher's true courage and goodness would purify the intellectual and moral force in him which was called the soul. For it was the goodness or badness of the soul which made a man good or bad, and thus happy or unhappy. Socrates clearly believed that everything in the world was arranged for the best, and that if human beings tried always, as a matter of religious duty, to make their souls as 'healthy' as they could, they would eventually attain their natural goodness.

Now it may be argued that in expressing this view Socrates ignored the common situation in which someone may know what is good and yet find himself unable to act rightly. The Roman poet, Ovid, writing in the first century AD summed it up thus: 'I see and approve of things which are better, but I follow the worse.' St Paul and many later thinkers understood the problem of the war that goes on in a man's mind between the good he should be aiming at and the evil he actually does. But the fact is that Socrates, towards the end of his life at any rate, seemed to find no difficulty in living up to his own high standards of behaviour. This means that, to many people, his views can give little help since they take no account of an inner conflict between right and wrong. And yet Socrates did become for a good number of philosophers in succeeding generations the model of the virtuous man.

The everlasting nature of the soul

From the problem of how to attain true goodness, Socrates passed to the question of learning. He insisted that what was known in the present was the recollection of something learned in the past. Our souls must all have had a previous existence before they became part of human beings; they were then independent of bodies and had intelligence. Although Socrates' friends were prepared to agree so far, there was some hesitation about accepting the suggestion that souls, as well as existing before men's births, also continued to exist after their deaths. They clearly did not want to think that he would go from them completely at the end of his life, and for that reason were anxious to find some satisfying explanation of what happened after death. For them, as for most intellectuals of their day, the traditional stories of the Underworld were meaningless. And yet they could not push the physical departure of their master out of their thoughts during those last hours together, and the finality of it seemed more real than anything else.

Socrates understood their difficulty. So he set about persuading them that there were absolute forms of things such as Beauty, forms that were eternal and unchanging, which could only be grasped by the mind. Examples of Beauty that could be appreciated by the senses must always be changing and variable. When he saw that they agreed, he made the point towards which he had been leading: in the same way, once the soul was freed from the body it could become divine and changeless. It could reach a place where it would find happiness and be released from all human ills and weaknesses.

THE TRANSMIGRATION OF SOULS

He added a warning, however. Sometimes souls were unable to break away completely as a result of too close a contact with physical things during life. Then they were dragged back into the visible world and, as ghosts of the wicked, hovered around tombs. The really evil might become perverse creatures like donkeys, or violent creatures like wolves. On the other hand, those who had tried in life to be good citizens might turn into bees, wasps or ants – creatures which had an awareness of some social responsibility – or might even be re-created in human form.

Such an idea was not original to Socrates or to Plato or to the Greeks. A religious sect associated with the legendary hero and musician, Orpheus, and also the followers of the mathematician-philosopher Pythagoras (who lived more than a hundred years before Socrates) had held the belief that the soul could be released from the prison of the body, but would then be subjected to a carefully planned system of rewards and punishments, of promotion and demotion.

As we have seen, Plato was almost certainly present at the trial of Socrates and recorded what was said there in the *Apology*. If we compare the ideas put forward in that work with those supposedly propounded by Socrates on his last day in prison – when Plato was absent – we find some inconsistency. Socrates had earlier made it clear that he felt his best way of attaining goodness and preparing for death was to discuss and examine questions of practical conduct with his fellow citizens. He did not at that time suggest that the philosopher should turn his eyes right away from the physical world, longing for the moment when his soul might escape. This change of approach might suggest that the views attributed to Socrates in the *Phaedo* were Plato's own, and that he felt justified in supporting his friend's faith with arguments which he himself found convincing.

29. *Orpheus*

THE OBJECTIONS OF SIMMIAS AND CEBES

Most of Socrates' companions were satisfied with his reasoning. But Simmias and Cebes could not yet accept that it had been proved that the soul was the eternal part of man. Socrates noticed that when he stopped talking they went on murmuring to each other for some time. Anxious, as ever, to encourage others to examine their own ideas, he urged them to voice their difficulties. Simmias answered:

'All right, Socrates. I'll be truthful. For a time now we've both had some doubts, and each of us has been pressing the other to ask

F

questions. We want to hear your answers but we hesitated to worry you in case it irritated you in your present situation.' When Socrates heard this he smiled and said, 'Really, Simmias, I shall certainly have difficulty in persuading other people that I don't think of my present situation as a calamity when I can't even convince you, and you are afraid that I am more short-tempered now than I was before.' [Plato, *Phaedo* 84 c]

Socrates went on to mention the popular belief about swans, that the only occasion on which they sang was just before death to express their sorrow. Their song was in no way a lament, he insisted, but a hymn of joy, by which the swans, which were sacred to Apollo and had prophetic powers, revealed their knowledge of the glories awaiting them in the unseen future world. He concluded:

> And I think that I am in some way a fellow-servant of the swans and dedicated to the same god. The prophetic powers given to me by my master are not inferior to theirs, and I am no more distressed at leaving life than they are. So if that is all you are worried about, you must speak out and ask anything you like in the time that the Eleven allow us.[1] [Plato, *Phaedo* 85 b]

Thus encouraged, Simmias and Cebes stated their difficulties. Simmias said that many believed that the body was held together at a certain tension between the extremes of hot and cold, wet and dry, and so on. The soul was the result of a combination and adjustment of these same extremes in exactly the right proportion. Obviously as soon as the tension of the body was altered (that is, by death), the soul must also be destroyed. What could be said to resolve that difficulty?

Before Socrates attempted a reply, he suggested that Cebes should indicate *his* problem. Cebes obliged – with an analogy. Suppose, he said, that an old tailor had just died. According to Socrates' reasoning, one would offer as proof of the old man's continued existence in some other world the fact that the coat he made for himself was still intact and had not perished with him. For the argument would run like this: a man was likely to last longer than his coat; so if the coat still existed, the tailor certainly would not have ceased to exist. But this was absurd. He would wear out many coats but would perish before the last one. Cebes thought that in the same way the soul was long-lived while the body was short-lived and weak. One soul might wear out many bodies, but eventually would perish before its final 'coat'. Therefore no one but a fool could be confident when facing death unless he had proved convincingly that the soul was absolutely indestructible.

[1] A reference to the Eleven Officers of Justice in Athens whose duties included responsibility for prisoners.

Socrates' calmness

This depressed everyone, although they had been persuaded by Socrates' previous arguments. However, he aroused their admiration again both by his quick understanding of the problems of Simmias and Cebes and by the skill with which he comforted his friends, while encouraging them to continue the argument. He teased Phaedo about the curls on his neck and said they would presumably be cut the next day as a sign of mourning. 'But not if you take my advice,' he added. 'Why not?' asked Phaedo. 'Because I shall cut my own hair *today*, and so should you, if our argument dies and we can't bring it to life again.' Thus by showing he could still joke about death, Socrates was able to cheer them up.

Now he warned them once more of the danger of giving up an inquiry, of 'quarrelling with philosophy' before they had attained the truth. And he reminded them that it was the finding of truth that was the most important thing. They must think far more about that and stop worrying about his approaching death. The discussion about the nature of the soul was then resumed and it was followed by a lengthy dissertation on the eternal Forms of things. This led once more to the question of the immortality of the soul. Socrates here emphasised the need for careful training of a man's soul if it was to enjoy its existence in the next world. But in order to appreciate what this next world would be like, everyone must first understand the true nature of the earth.

A DESCRIPTION OF THE EARTH

This is part of a description that Socrates gave of the earth:

> I believe it is very large and that those of us who live between the Pillars of Hercules and the River Phasis only inhabit a tiny part of it (round the Mediterranean) like ants or frogs round a pond, and that there are many other people living in similar places. Round the earth there are everywhere hollows of every shape and size into which water and mist and air have collected. [Plato, *Phaedo* 109 b]

By the 'Pillars of Hercules' the Ancient World meant the Straits of Gibraltar, which were generally believed to be the western edge of the earth. The River Phasis, which flowed into the Black Sea, was the traditional north-eastern boundary of civilisation.

We have in recent years heard astronauts flying in space exclaim at the extraordinarily beautiful colours that met their eyes. Socrates told his friends that if man could leave the 'hollows' in which he lived and, putting on wings, fly aloft, he would see the real earth that lay beneath the heavens:

> If it were seen from above, it is said it would look like a ball made of twelve pieces of leather of different colours, of which the colours we have here are only mere suggestions, like the paints which artists use; in fact, the whole earth is composed of such colours, and others much brighter and much purer still. One part is a magnificent purple, another golden; everything white is whiter than snow or chalk. And the rest is composed of other colours in the same way, more numerous and more beautiful than any we have seen. Even the actual hollows in the earth which are filled with water and air take on a kind of colour of their own as they shine among the varied hues around them, with the result that there appears to be one unbroken surface of different colours. [Plato, *Phaedo* 110 c]

THE WORLD BELOW

But the subject of death could not be avoided for long, and Socrates went on to describe his idea of the Underworld, the world of the dead, where the souls of good and bad were judged and allocated final dwelling places. He admitted that no sensible man would insist that the facts were exactly as he described them, but he believed an account like his should be used to give confidence about the life to come. All his friends would at some time have to face the journey to the next world. For him the hour was now at hand:

> It is getting on for the time when I must drink the poison. I'd like to have a bath first, so that the women don't have the trouble of washing me after I am dead. [Plato, *Phaedo* 115 a]

When Socrates had finished speaking, Crito asked for final instructions about the care of Xanthippe and the children. What could his friends do at the last to please him? But there were no new directions. All that was necessary, Socrates insisted, was that they should not fail to follow the pattern of life he had given them. As for methods of burial which Crito was worrying about – what happened to the physical body was of no importance whatsoever. They could bury him in any way they liked. And he added lightly: 'That is, if you can get hold of me and I don't slip from your grasp.' In other words, the real Socrates would by then be gone.

The drinking of the poison

While Crito accompanied him to his bath, Socrates' other friends remained behind, thinking about all that had been discussed that day, and bewailing the calamity which was befalling them. They felt, said Phaedo afterwards, as though they were losing a father and would be orphans for the rest of their lives.

For the last time Socrates' three sons came with the women of his household to see him. There were no dramatic scenes of farewell. With Crito still beside him, he gave them a few instructions and then sent them away.

He had only just returned to his friends when the gaoler arrived to warn him that it was time to drink the poison:

> 'Socrates,' he said, 'I shall not have to reproach you, as I do others because they get angry with me and swear at me when, following Government orders, I tell them to drink the poison. I've discovered during this time that you're the noblest and gentlest and the bravest of all those who have ever come here. And I'm quite sure that you're not angry with me; for others, as you are well aware, are to blame, and not me. So now, goodbye – you know why I have come; and try to bear lightly what has to be.' As he said this, he burst into tears, turned and went out. Socrates looked up and said, 'Goodbye. I'll do what you say.' Then to us he added, 'What a courteous man! All the time I've been in prison he's visited me and sometimes had a talk with me, and has been most kind; and how generous of him to weep on my account.' [Plato, *Phaedo* 116 c, d]

Crito urged Socrates not to have the poison brought yet, saying he knew that often condemned prisoners enjoyed a dinner and the company of friends long after they received the warning from the gaoler. But he might have known what the reply would be. Socrates gently rebuked him for suggesting that there was any profit in clinging to life when it had nothing more to offer. He would only make himself ridiculous in his own eyes if he did that.

So Crito sent out his slave to fetch the officer who was to administer the poison. It was all ready mixed in a cup. Socrates asked for instructions. The officer told him that all he had to do was to walk about until his legs felt heavy and then to lie down, and the poison would act of its own accord. At the same time he handed the cup to Socrates, who very cheerfully and without trembling, without even a change of expression, looked the man full in the face, as his manner was, took the cup and asked his permission to pour a drink-offering out of it to the gods. The officer explained that the amount had been carefully measured and there would not be enough. Socrates accepted this, but said that he had to ask the gods for a safe journey to the next world. So he prayed and, raising the cup to his lips, calmly and without distaste, drained it.

It was then that his friends broke down. They had kept their self-control fairly well so far, although Crito had had to go out as he could not restrain his tears. Now one of them, Apollodorus, who had been weeping all the time, burst into such a flood of tears that all who were there broke down except Socrates, who reproached them for behaving just as he had feared the womenfolk would. They were ashamed at that and regained control of themselves.

The death of Socrates

Socrates began to walk about, and when his legs felt heavy he lay down as instructed. The officer who had given him the poison, after looking at his feet and legs from time to time, then pressed his foot hard and asked if there were any feeling in it. Socrates said no. The man did the same to his legs, moving his hands gradually up Socrates' body as it grew cold and stiff. Then he felt him again and said that when the poison reached his heart he would die. As the effect of it spread to his abdomen, Socrates uncovered his face – he had covered it up as he lay there – and spoke his last words: 'Crito, I owe a cock to Asclepius. Will you remember to offer it for me?' [Plato, *Phaedo* 118 a]

30. *Asclepius*

The reference to a cock meant one of two things. It was either an offering made by patients at the shrine of Asclepius, the god of healing, before they went to sleep in the temple grounds, in the hope that it would cause the god to cure them by the time they awoke; or it was a customary thank-offering when a cure had been effected. By either interpretation, Socrates was probably implying that death was the cure for the sickness of life. There was no reply to Crito's last question, 'Is there anything else you want done?' Shortly afterwards, Socrates made a convulsive movement and the officer uncovered him. His eyes were set, and Crito, seeing this, closed his eyes and mouth.

'Such,' said Phaedo, 'was the death of our friend – a man who I can truly say was of all those of his time that I knew the best, the wisest, and the most just.'

8

The Influence of Socrates

Socrates' influence on his contemporaries

SOCRATES had never claimed to be a great thinker. He had admitted his
own ignorance and had seen himself only as a stinging fly sent to stir
others into mental activity and self-questioning. He left no books which
men could study after his death. What he did have however was, quite
clearly, a magnetic personality. This, together with remarkable intellectual
powers, enabled him to make people listen when he talked. Alcibiades
is made to say of him in Plato's *Symposium* that when he listened to
Pericles or any other excellent speakers he recognised that they spoke
well, but his soul was not disturbed by them or filled with self-reproach;
but when anyone listened to Socrates, or even heard his words indifferently
repeated by another, he was deeply moved and it was as though a spell
had been cast over him. Yet perhaps it was not in the end so much what
Socrates said as the standards by which he lived which influenced those
who knew him. As we have seen, he insisted on following where his
conscience led, even if it meant his death at the command of the State.
For he accepted that Athens had the right to demand his obedience to
her laws.

Socrates taught his followers to question and argue, to use discussion
as a means of reaching the truth, and always to seek 'the Good'. Exactly
what he meant by 'the Good' he did not always make clear and it was
therefore the task of some of his immediate successors to attempt a
definition of it. We have already considered how Plato – in addition to
recording what Socrates said – interpreted the results of his teaching and
tried in a number of dialogues to reinforce it so that it would stand up to
criticism. His pupil Aristotle carried this process a stage further and, in
doing so, turned many of Socrates' (or Plato's) conclusions on their
head.

ARISTOTLE

Aristotle was born fifteen years after Socrates' death. He came to Athens

Aristotle

31.

when he was seventeen to become a pupil of Plato, and remained a member of the latter's 'school', the Academy, for about twenty years, studying, writing and teaching. After Plato's death he left the Academy and with some friends settled first near the coast of Asia Minor and then at Mitylene on the island of Lesbos. From there he was invited by Philip, King of Macedon, to be the tutor of his thirteen-year-old son, later to be known as Alexander the Great.

Aristotle wrote a large number of books. From those which have survived it is possible to see how his ideas evolved. At first he was a true follower of Plato, then he began to criticise him and finally adopted an independent attitude and method in his philosophical teaching. Aristotle would not have been personally interested in Socrates, nor was he emotionally involved in his life or death as Plato, Xenophon or many others were. Instead, he was able to look calmly and critically at Socrates' teaching and often reached totally opposed conclusions. For example, he could not accept the view that no one intentionally acted wrongly. Socrates had maintained that men were courageous only because they knew that whatever might happen to them could not be bad if it brought more benefit to the soul than cowardly behaviour would. This, Aristotle argued, made no allowance for man's lack of self-control, and clearly contradicted experience. Someone doing wrong might well know the universal rule about it, but be more affected by the particular circumstances in which he acted. It would be with the senses that he would perceive each situation, and this 'sense-perception' was not, to Aristotle, true knowledge. So he began like this with much of Socrates' teaching as it had been interpreted by Plato, and moved on from there to his own philosophy.

ANTISTHENES AND ARISTIPPUS

Many of Socrates' friends and pupils themselves engaged in teaching, developing some of his ideas and concentrating on one or two of them to the exclusion of others. Some of them became the founders of new 'schools' of philosophy, and many stories were collected about them. Two examples will show how such men, while much affected by their contact with Socrates, differed from him in the emphasis of their teaching.

Antisthenes, one of Socrates' most devoted followers, was said to have walked five miles every day into Athens in order to listen to him. What impressed him most about Socrates was his complete lack of interest in material possessions and wordly pleasures – so that goodness might be pursued without distraction. For instance, Socrates wore a tattered cloak because he believed there were more important matters than fine clothes to think about. As a result, Antisthenes and his school developed what amounted to a cult of poverty. One day Antisthenes deliberately adjusted his cloak so that the torn part of it was clearly visible. Instead of the praise he was expecting, he received a rebuke from Socrates who commented, 'I can see your vanity through your cloak'. This story may well be a later invention, but at least it illustrates the difference between a genuine disregard of the unimportant on the part of Socrates and a flaunting of asceticism on the part of some of his followers.

Diogenes Laertius, who related the story in his *Lives and Beliefs of Eminent Philosophers* (already referred to in Chapter 5) had another about Socrates' close friend, Aristippus of Cyrene. Aristippus had come to Athens because of Socrates' reputation as a teacher, and is said to have been the first of his friends and pupils to charge professional fees. He became sufficiently well known to be invited to join the court of Dionysius I at Syracuse in Sicily, where he apparently enjoyed a life of luxury, teaching that bodily pleasures should be everyone's aim. When accused of deserting Socrates' principles, he replied, 'I went to Socrates for education, to Dionysius for amusement.' He insisted that he did not mean a man to be overcome by his pleasures, but rather that he should guide them as he wished, just as he might control a horse or a ship. To Socrates, as we have seen, mastery of himself had necessitated leading a temperate life. Aristippus, even though moving far from that position, still, as it were, echoed Socrates' voice when he concentrated on the study of good and evil and the happiness of human beings.

Who was Socrates?

Many writers have stated that the solution to the problem of the 'historical Socrates' can never be found, nor can the search for his true meaning ever be ended. We began with the portraits of him that Plato, Xenophon and Aristophanes provided – contradictory portraits in a number of ways, but all contributing to our understanding of him. If they had been identical, we might well be suspicious that we were being given a very one-sided view. Although Socrates offended many people, he was devotedly loved by his close friends, who found him an entertaining and kindly companion, an inspiring talker and a man of great intellectual ability. We can also say that what established his influence among his contemporaries and immediate successors was his strong moral feeling, together with his readiness to meet disagreement and criticism. In general, he can be said to epitomise the problem faced by so many in all ages from his own time up to the present day – the conflict between the individual and the State, the struggle for freedom of conscience along with respect for law and order.

Socrates' life and ideas impressed many Roman writers, some of whom made rather exaggerated claims about him, thus contributing to the myth which had quickly grown up around him after his death. Cicero, statesman, orator and man of letters, wrote in the first century BC:

> Judging by the evidence of every man of learning and by the opinion of the Greeks in general, we may say that Socrates was outstanding for his good sense, his eloquence, his charming manner and the breadth and quality of his argument, whatever he might be discussing.
> [Cicero, *De Oratore* III 16, 60]

Aristophanes in the *Clouds* had represented Socrates swinging in his

32.

basket in the air, unable and unwilling to do his thinking at ground level among ordinary human beings. In contrast to this, Cicero described him thus:

> Socrates was the first man to bring philosophy down from the heavens and set her firmly in cities on earth, bringing her into the homes of the people, and making them consider their lives and their standards of behaviour. [Cicero, *Fragments* v 4, 10]

84

To Seneca, a philosopher who in 49 AD was appointed tutor to the boy who was to become the emperor Nero, Socrates represented the ideal man:

> If you want a model, look at Socrates, a strong old man, battling against all the storms of life, refusing to be overwhelmed by poverty or hard work. He lived during a period of war, under dictatorship or anarchy. . . . At last he was condemned on very serious charges, accused of teaching against the State religion and corrupting the minds of the young. Then came imprisonment and death by poison. Yet none of this disturbed him. To the end no one ever saw him depressed. Wonderful! Magnificent! Unique! [Seneca, *Letters* 104, 27]

Dio Chrysostom, a writer on political and philosophical subjects, who lived in Rome at about the same time as Seneca, commented:

> The words of Socrates survive and always will, although he wrote nothing and left no work or testament. [Dio Chrysostom, 54, 3]

And another contemporary, the Greek biographer Plutarch, who produced a work called *On the Genius of Socrates* as well as making frequent references to him in other books, wrote:

> His criticisms of other people were more successful because he did not himself make definite assertions about things. He seemed to be sharing with others in a search for truth, rather than putting them right with some ready-made statement of fact. He had medical skill which was not used to heal the body, but to cure the diseased and poisoned soul. [Plutarch, *Questions about Plato* 999 c]

About two hundred years later, Julian, the Roman Emperor who was known as the Apostate because he rebelled against the influence of Christianity and tried to restore paganism, said of Socrates:

> I assert that his achievements were more glorious than those of Alexander the Great. In my opinion he embodied the wisdom of Plato, the military ability of Xenophon, the toughness of Antisthenes, and the philosophies of Cebes, Simmias, Phaedo and hundreds of others, as well as those of the 'schools' which developed as a result of their teaching – the Lyceum, the Stoa, the Academy. Everyone who now owes his salvation to philosophy owes it to Socrates. [Julian, *Letters* 264 b]

But does any of this provide a satisfactory explanation of the power that Socrates exerted over his contemporaries and over so many others in subsequent generations? Who, indeed, was Socrates? We may not feel we can say with Phaedo that he was 'of all men the best, the wisest and the most just'. We might want to treat with reserve Xenophon's 'I cannot help writing about him, nor, as I write, help praising him'. But is it just possible that Socrates' own maxim, 'the unexamined life is not worth living', may provide the best memorial to his career and go a little way towards revealing the man beneath the myth?

Socrates

33.

Index